THE
EASY ART
OF
SMOKING
FOOD

THE
EASY ART
—— OF ——
SMOKING
FOOD

Chris Dubbs
and
Dave Heberle

Illustrations by Jay Marcinowski
Photographs by Gary Thomas Sutto

Winchester Press

Library of Congress Cataloging in Publication Data

Dubbs, Chris.
  The easy art of smoking food.

  Includes index.
  1. Meat, Smoked.   2. Fish, Smoked.
I. Heberle, Dave, joint author.   II. Title.
TX609.D8   641.4'6   77-4893
ISBN 0-87691-243-9 Second Printing
ISBN: 0-87691-264-1 (PAPER EDITION) First printing   1977

WINCHESTER is a Trademark of Olin Corporation used by
Winchester Press, Inc. under authority and control of the
Trademark Proprietor

Printed in the United States of America

Published by Winchester Press
205 East 42nd Street
New York, N.Y. 10017

CONTENTS

CHAPTER I

HISTORY

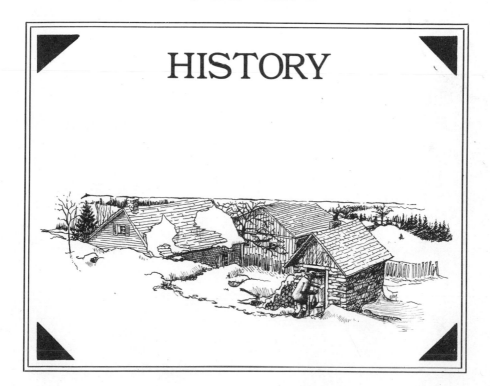

The history of preserving food is a long and cloudy one. Eons ago, the struggle for survival was largely a matter of man eating anything that didn't eat him. Foods were neither grown nor cooked—let alone preserved.

But the years brought man weapons and caves—and fire, which became the primary means of cooking and preserving food. The first primitive recipes would hardly be appreciated today, as the only ingredient was fresh-killed game and the only instruction to throw it in the fire.

Slowly, the practice of preserving food became more sophisticated. By the dawn of civilization, when there were already 200,000,000 mouths to feed, the elementary forms of food preservation—pickling, salting, and smoking—were already being practiced.

Smoking was eventually to establish itself as one of the most convenient and reliable methods of preserving meat for long storage. It was no surprise, therefore, that smoking became an integral part of Colonial America. Almost every home had a separate smokehouse and many cabins had smoke holes incorporated within their chimneys, where meat could be suspended and smoked using the cabin hearth as the source for the smoke and heat.

The popularity of smoking remained relatively stable until 1803, when a Baltimore, Maryland, man placed a small carton covered with insulation within another box. He stored ice and food inside and called the contraption a "refrigerator." This new, more convenient method of storing food caught on rapidly.

The icebox, the freezer, modern methods of processing meat, all these conspired against the age-old custom of home smoking. Since fresh meat from the Midwest could be shipped east daily in refrigerated cars, and freezers could keep food fresh for months on end, operating a smokehouse seemed an unnecessary bother.

Although food smoking faded from view for many years, it was never in any danger of dying out completely. Many foods just tasted too good when smoked—bacon, for example, and ham, sausage, and all kinds of fish, especially salmon. The smoking of food moved into the big commercial smokehouses. The availability of smoked food became a problem, and what was available was often of dubious quality, filled with chemical preservatives and coloring and even "artificial smoke flavor."

Home smoking held on through the years mostly among enthusiastic sportsmen, who would fabricate smokers out of old refrigerators, barrels, garages, wheelbarrows, anything—just so they could enjoy the fresh smoked flavor of fish and game.

Within the last five years, the portable, electric smoker has grown in popularity, helping to spark a revival in food smoking. Because of its convenience and modest price, this appliance is returning food smoking to the masses.

In spite of this renewed interest in food smoking, there has been a scarcity of information on the subject, amounting almost to a conspiracy over the last decade. It is as if no one is supposed to know how to make delicious smoked salmon or succulent, sugar-cured hams. Published information has often been conflicting. Most magazine articles seemed to imply that their instructions were only relevant at a campfire in the mountains or in a garbage-can smoker. No wonder more people weren't smoking food!

One thing that was clear in all the jumbled, distorted information of the past was that many people were smoking food in many different ways and all were apparently satisfied with the results. If nothing else, it indicated that smoking is hardly an exact science. Smoking food is, in fact, an art. A great many variables influence the flavor of the finished product and most of them are under the control of the person doing the smoking. Fortunately for everyone who enjoys the unique flavor of smoked foods, smoking is an easy art.

Beneath all the individualized approaches are but a few simple procedures that anyone can master in short order. Working within these guidelines, the novice smoker can produce an astonishing array of masterfully smoked foods, turning even lowly, inexpensive cuts of meat into gourmet fare.

The Easy Art of Smoking Food is written with the idea that smoking food is something anyone can do. Every effort has been made to simplify and modernize age-old recipes and procedures without compromising quality. Since it was the electric smoker that brought the art back to the people, many instructions are written with that appliance in mind. Each recipe and procedure, however, is applicable or easily adapted to any other smoking device.

One thing a book on smoking cannot do is give precisely detailed instructions. Personal taste and smoker idiosyncracies are the two biggest reasons, but there are a host of factors that influence how you handle a particular meat, some of which may change each time you smoke. What is the size or the cut of the meat? Is it to be eaten immediately or put in storage? How much time do you have to prepare it? Does it need tenderizing? What method of cooking is to be used before or after smoking? How much salt flavor do you prefer? How much smoke flavor? These are only some of the factors involved.

A set of instructions appropriate for one occasion might be all wrong for the next. Obviously, instructions cannot be provided for every possible combination of circumstances. Therefore, most directions throughout this book are given in ranges. For instance, smoking or curing times might be given as "one to four hours." This is usually done to provide a range of flavor from mild to strong. When uncertain about your taste preferences, it is always best to start with the shortest time. If you then desire a stronger flavor, the meat can be returned for additional smoking or you can increase the time on your next effort.

The equipment you use will also determine how you apply the instructions of this book. Sometimes smoking times and temperatures may seem unnecessarily ambiguous, but this is partly to account for differences in smokers. The fact is, not all smokers produce the same amount of heat. Makeshift smokers, especially, vary in the temperatures they are capable of producing and sustaining. Portable, electric smokers will be influenced by outside air temperatures.

To allow for personal taste and equipment performance, numerous methods of smoking have been detailed for each kind and cut of meat. You need only select the procedure that best suits your needs and the circumstances.

The key to finding true happiness with your smoker is to experiment. Producing good smoked food is easy; producing great smoked food takes a little imagination. Hints are provided throughout the book on how to vary taste with cures, marinades, seasoning, and smoking times. Use these suggestions as guidelines. As you gain experience, you will quickly learn that the time ranges and recipes here provided in no sense represent the total possible ways of smoking food—that uncharted, gastronomic universe can only be determined by you.

THE SMOKING PROCESS

Smoldering hard wood is the source of smoke in a food smoker. Borne on the vapors of smoke are countless microscopic droplets of chemicals, the most important of which are aldehydes, phenols, ketones, and acetic acid. These chemicals, released from the burning wood, are instrumental in killing yeast, mold, and bacteria, and retarding their future growth. As a supply of fresh smoke circulates around food in a smoker, these components are deposited on the surface and absorbed into the moisture of the food. Moisture allows the chemicals to penetrate the food, distributing their preservative and flavoring effects.

Food is also affected by the hot air accompanying smoke. Even at room temperatures, food loses moisture. This loss is greatly accelerated at the higher temperatures associated with smoking. Partial dehydration is an important part of the preservative function of smoking. If there is no moisture in food, bacterial growth is practically nil and food does not spoil.

Many foodstuffs have a surprisingly high moisture content, as much as 80 percent in some fish. By using low temperatures, smoking can greatly reduce the moisture content of meat without cooking it. Aside from offering protection against spoilage, this also tends to make the nutrients in the meat more concentrated.

Cold Smoking and Hot Smoking

The temperatures inside most modern smokers will range anywhere from the temperature of the outside air up to 225°F. Smokehouses that existed years ago operated at relatively low temperatures, usually below 120°F. At such low temperatures, food only accumulates the beneficial effects of smoke without actually cooking. As with old-fashioned hams, meat could remain at these smokehouse temperatures for several days and would still require cooking before being eaten.

When smoker temperatures climb above 120°F., meat is partially cooked as it smokes. At the somewhat higher temperatures of 170°F. or 190°F., it is entirely feasible to cook meat completely in a smoker; 120°F. is the rather arbitrary division between the two different types of smoking. The lower temperatures are referred to as "cold smoking" and the higher temperatures as "hot smoking" or "smoke cooking."

In the past, lengthy periods of cold smoking were an important method of processing meat to be stored for a long time without refrigeration. Today, the preservative quality of cold smoking has taken a back seat to its flavoring capabilities. When placed in a cold smoke, meat will quickly acquire a smoke flavor. This makes cold smoking a useful supplement to the regular kitchen preparation of meat. Without complicated alteration of cooking time, meat can be given the exotic flavor of smoke, either before or after cooking.

Smoke cooking is a relatively recent development. It combines smoke flavoring with cooking for greater convenience. This method is possible on almost any makeshift smoker in which the source of heat is in the same compartment as the food. Hot smoking has only truly come of age with the advent of the electric smoker, which generally provides for higher and more stable temperatures.

CHAPTER II

SMOKERS
AND
THEIR FUELS

In the wilderness, it may be a gridwork of sticks above a campfire; a handyman might build himself a plywood shack; manufacturers offer a variety of electric models. Whatever alternative you choose, acquiring a smoker is your first move if you want to smoke food.

The creative ingenuity that private individuals have expanded in the development of the makeshift smoker has been phenomenal. Many of them work as well as, or better than, commercially available units. If you're a do-it-yourselfer, this chapter will provide you with details on some of the more successful homemade smokers.

Of course, you can also buy one. Portable electric smokers are now widely available in sporting goods and hardware stores. Their efficiency, reliability, ease of handling, and modest price make them an ideal investment for home smoking.

Each one of the following smokers has its advantages and disadvantages. Consider your circumstances and your smoking needs and choose the one that's right for you.

ELECTRIC SMOKERS

If you buy an electric smoker, study the directions included. The first piece of advice should be to break in your new appliance with a dry run by burning several pans of wood without actually smoking any food. This will impart a smoke aroma to the inside of the smoker and eliminate all chances of tainting your first batch of smokables with a metallic or paint flavor.

An electric smoker will not only smoke food, it will also smoke-cook food. Old-time smoking processes required extended smoking periods of days or even weeks; the electric smoker speeds things up considerably by cooking meat as it adds the distinctive flavor of smoke. In this day and age, when time is at a premium, an electric smoker will provide quality products as

Interior of a portable electric smoker. The pan of sawdust rests on the heating element; the tray at bottom catches the dripping grease. Food is placed on racks or suspended from hooks at the top.

Ventilation controls temperature in an electric smoker. Ventilator flap on left also provides access to the fuel pan. On unit on right, the entire door raises and lowers.

customized and as mouth-watering as those meticulously prepared by long-gone generations, and for a surprisingly minimal time investment.

A typical electric smoker consists of:

A smoke box of aluminum or steel. Aluminum won't rust, but then it's not quite as sturdy as steel. You have a choice of several sizes, the largest of which will accommodate a medium-size ham or a heavy turkey.

A ceramic or metal heating element. Installed at the base of the smoker, the heating element provides temperatures hot enough to singe wood fuels into smoke and to help cook food.

A vent at the base to provide draft control and heat regulation, and vents that allow stale smoke to escape at the smoker's top. These latter also make convenient thermometer check holes.

A tray to catch drippings; food racks; hooks for suspending items such as sausages; and a pan to hold fuel over the heating element.

Even though the electric heating element generates a uniform heat, inside temperatures can be made to vary by regulating the air vent. In some models, the entire smoker door slides upward to provide an opening; in others, there is a louvered flap. Closing the flap or door conserves heat; opening it allows cooler outside air to enter.

Open door or not, outside air will significantly affect the inside temperature of any smoker. Most electric smokers are used in the outdoors—on patios, balconies, or in garages—where air temperatures will fluctuate. Their use inside the house is not recommended, primarily because they give off that "campfire" odor that everyone loves—everyone except whoever is responsible for housekeeping; for it clings to curtains and infiltrates the entire home.

Electric smokers have nothing in the way of insulation to conserve heat. To smoke a fish in the summertime, when the weather is balmy, you may have to open the air vent and let some heat escape just to keep temperatures from climbing too high. If you're smoking that same fish in winter, you'll have to keep the vent closed to retain as much heat as possible, and you still might not get up to the desired temperature. A word of caution: Never shut all doors and vents so smoke is completely trapped inside. Smoke confined too long becomes dead and stale and will give food a bitter taste.

Electric models do have some other drawbacks. They cannot process large quantities and they always require electricity. If you want to smoke in the backyard, far from your house, the use of a long extension cord will reduce the amount of heat generated in the unit's heating element.

HOMEMADE SMOKERS

Successful smokers of the homemade type have three common characteristics.

1. *A smoke box*. Something to contain smoke long enough to impart the smoke flavor to food. As the following pages suggest, the smoke box can be a cardboard box, an old refrigerator, a wooden shanty, or what-have-you.

2. *A heat and smoke source*. Something to generate heat and smoke, such as an electric hot plate. This is convenient when used with small smokers, doesn't require much tending, and provides even, uninterrupted heat. Or a small pile of burning charcoal briquettes, on which wood chips are burned. Briquettes last a considerable amount of time, and provide relatively even heat. They take a while to start, however. Or you can use a fire can, probably the best heat and smoke source for larger units. All it amounts to is a metal can, preferably with a handle, half full of hardwood chunks, with a metal lid to regulate how much oxygen is admitted to the fire and how fast and hot the wood burns. The size of the fire can will depend on the size of the smoker. A three-pound coffee can may suffice for small units; larger ones will need a bucket or a five- or ten-gallon can.

3. *Food trays and hooks*. Anything to keep the food toward the top of the smoker, suspended over the heat and smoke source. Screens, racks, metal trays, or hooks are all useful.

SMOKEHOUSES AND COLD SMOKERS

The purpose of the old-fashioned smokehouse was to preserve meat. This meant very slow smoking, with little heat, for as long as several weeks. To accomplish this, smokehouses had the source of heat outside the compartment in which the meat hung. Smoke was conducted, through a pipe or ditch, from the fire to the smoking compartment thus dissipating practically all

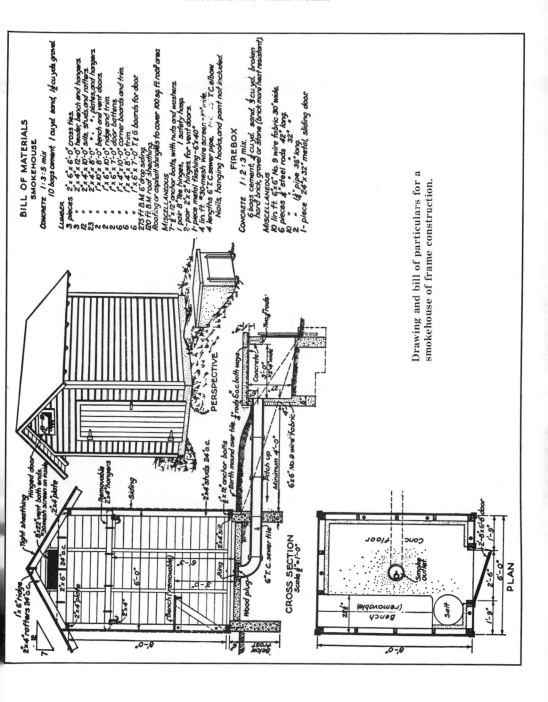

Drawing and bill of particulars for a smokehouse of frame construction.

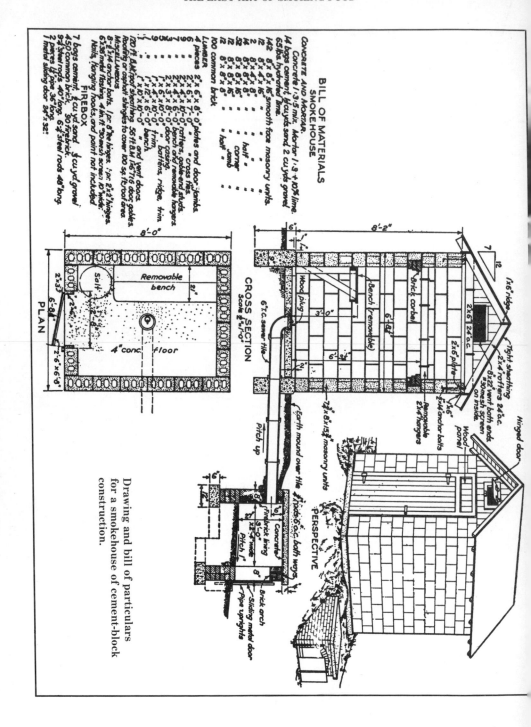

Drawing and bill of particulars for a smokehouse of cement-block construction.

heat. If you consider building one of these, you should be aware that you will only be able to cold-smoke food, and many of the procedures described in this book call for temperatures higher than those smokehouses can obtain.

Because smokehouses have served, and continue to serve, the needs of many people, several designs are included here. A cold smoker is simply a smaller version of the smokehouse.

Wooden Smokers

To envision the kind of wooden smoker you want, use your imagination and whatever materials you have on hand. You can construct a plywood smoker of any size, depending upon the quantity of food you're planning to process and the size of your yard. With a heavy smoking schedule and plenty of room, you might consider a shedlike setup with inside dimensions about six feet high by six feet square.

The inside should be lined with thin sheets of metal—tin or aluminum for instance. The metal sheathing helps reflect the heat and shortens smoking times and also keeps the plywood from disintegrating and curling from the high inside temperatures. A hinged walk-in set of double doors will facilitate easy loading and tending.

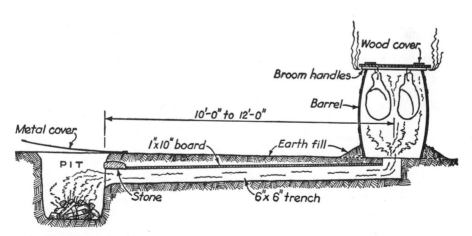

A pit-and-barrel cold smoker. Stovepipe or tile can be used for the flue. Smoking temperatures are low in this type of smoker.

Interior of a shed-type smoker. Fish hang several feet above firecan. Note the baffle plate, above the can, which regulates the amount of air getting to the burning wood and thus controls the temperature.

A five- or ten-gallon fire can, half full of fist-size chunks of hardwood, makes an ideal heat and smoke source. A metal lid or "heat-regulating baffle" should be attached above the can. Adjusting the lid will closely regulate the fire in the can: Close the lid to choke the oxygen supply and the fire will slow and produce less heat; open the lid to increase the oxygen and the fire will burn faster and hotter.

Sundry pieces of wooden furniture, such as a dresser, may also be remodeled into smokers. Knock the bottoms out of the top drawers and replace them with chicken wire or metal screening to convert the upper wooden compartments into handy pull-out food trays. Or, leave out the chicken wire, attach several hooks at the top, and you'll be able to handle turkeys, hams, or sausages. The bottoms should also be removed from the lower drawers to make room for a fire can. Drill several holes through the sides of the dresser, near the top, to release stale smoke.

Chests, trunks—practically anything—can be transformed into a satisfactory smoker. The only wood item you should not

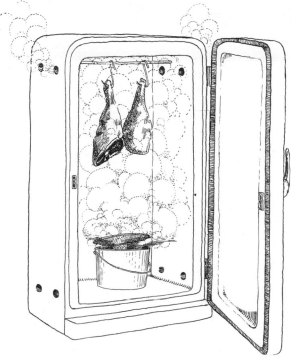

Refrigerator converted
to smoker.

use as a hot smoker is a barrel. The staves will dry out, shrink, and open.

Refrigerator Smokers

An old, one-door refrigerator may be converted into a very efficient smoker. Your newspaper's classified section may lead you to one or you might salvage one from a junk yard or dump. It shouldn't set you back more than fifteen dollars.

Haul the fridge home and remove the door's latch so that small children cannot trap themselves inside. Take out the motor below and the freezer compartment above. Remove all plastic and rubber fittings so they won't melt during high-temperature smoking. Cut one or two small holes near the top to serve as a smoke release, and drill several small holes near the bottom for draft. (Any small electric drill might serve, but if using a manual brace and bit, you might do best to supply yourself with metal instead of wood bits.) Rig up some sort of adjustable covering for the bottom vent holes to control draft. Secure hooks to the top for hanging.

19

Your heat and smoke source can be either an electric hot plate or a fire can. Never build a fire directly on the bottom of the refrigerator, as you don't know what kind of insulation is contained within; it might possibly catch fire and burn. Never allow the heat source to come in contact with exposed insulation.

A refrigerator-smoker has a lot going for it. It's well insulated and able to hold considerable heat, thereby shortening smoking times. (Nevertheless, use a thermometer to guard against excessive heat; a refrigerator simply wasn't built to withstand oven temperatures.) It has a full-length door for easy loading. It contains removable metal shelves that make convenient food trays. There is plenty of room to hang large items like hams or turkeys. And an old refrigerator is inexpensive and easy to convert.

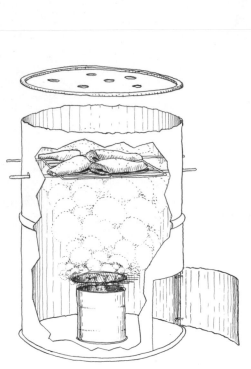

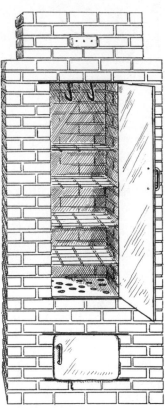

Drum smoker.

Masonry smoker.

Drum Smoker

Another makeshift unit very popular with smoking enthusiasts is the fifty-gallon drum.

First, clean the inside *thoroughly*, eliminating all traces of paint, oil, or whatever the drum held. Next, cut a small door near the bottom of the barrel to serve as a draft control and firecan access. Cut holes in the sides, near the top, in which to attach food trays. A stick or old broom handle can be laid across the top and supplied with hooks to support large items. Keep the cover and place it loosely over the drum's opening to hold in the smoke, being sure to leave some small opening near the top to allow smoke to escape.

A small fire can is probably the best heat source, but an electric hot plate may also be used.

A similar smoker can be made from a (preferably brand new) metal garbage can.

Masonry or Stone Smokers

Masonry and stone smokers are the Cadillacs of the smoker line. They're constructed in a manner identical to smokers made of other materials, but they're built to last, and often constructed much more elaborately. They won't rust, rot, or fall apart, and they have a way of almost blending into a rural setting as if they were part of the land.

Frequently smokers are incorporated into elaborate barbequeing units. After all, if you're going to all the trouble of constructing such an edifice, you might as well build it for maximum utilization.

The basic components of a masonry smoker are:

1. A fire box at the bottom, preferably with a sliding metal door to act as a draft control.

2. A metal plate, with holes directly above the fire box, that serves as a baffle, distributing smoke throughout the main chamber where food hangs.

3. The smoking chamber. It should be closed in on three sides. Supports should be fastened to the sides to hold food trays. A metal door, the length of the chamber, will make food loading easy. The door should have a seal of some noncombustible material, such as asbestos or furnace cement.

4. Holes at the top to allow for smoke escape.

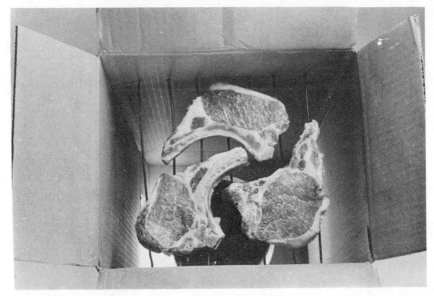

Top view of a cardboard smoker. Pieces of coat hangers provide the rack. Smoke is produced as wood burns on charcoal briquettes.

Cardboard Smoker

If you'd like to conduct a few experiments with food smoking before you actually build or buy your own smoker, find yourself a heavy cardboard box and make a temporary unit according to the following instructions.

Open the flaps at both ends and tape one set so the box can stand upright on them. Then, by sticking skewers, pieces of wire coat hangers, or sticks through the sides several inches below the top flaps, you can make a suitable rack on which to rest the food to be smoked.

Charcoal briquettes make an excellent heat source. Stack a few either on the ground or in a metal plate or tin can. The obvious concern with this type of smoker is to keep it from burning. A shallow hole can be dug in the ground to set the briquettes farther from the box. Usually there is no problem if the briquettes, or the container in which they burn, are kept from touching the cardboard.

After wood chips have been added to the heat source, set the box, taped flaps down, over the whole works. Place the food on the racks, then close the top flaps and keep them shut with a heavy weight. If your cardboard smoker is working properly, smoke will curl out from the top edges.

Occasionally sprinkle water on the bottom of the carton to keep the cardboard from igniting.

You can also use a cardboard smoker on overnight camping or fishing trips to smoke your catch along the stream or in the back woods. When finished, simply burn the box.

Stick Smokers

Stick smokers are spur-of-the-moment constructions used primarily on hunting trips when you don't have access to normal tools and facilities. For instance, if you're in upper Canada and you've bagged an elk and you want a good way of preserving the

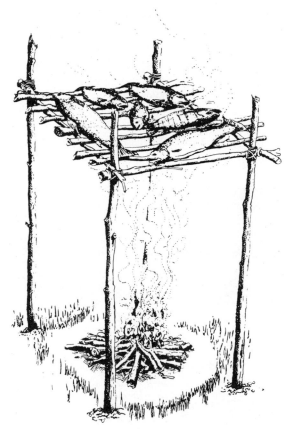

Stick smoker.

meat for the long haul home, then the stick smoker may be just what you need.

Cut four branches that are about five feet long and an inch and a half thick. Cut a point on one end, then drive the sticks, point down, into the ground around a small campfire. Lash four smaller sticks to the poles to form a square about three to four feet off the ground. Lay other sticks over these crosspieces to serve as a rack.

Build a small fire and fuel it with green wood to keep up a volume of smoke while holding down temperature. The height of the food above the fire can be varied. To preserve meat keep it away from the fire, allowing it to dry out from the smoke and low heat. The lower the rack, the greater the tendency for meat to cook.

The final step is to cover the framework with a blanket, tarpaulin, plastic, or even boughs—anything that can serve to contain the smoke.

SMOKER MAINTENANCE

Regardless of the type of smoker you use, about the only maintenance necessary is to keep it clean. There will naturally be grease from meat that is hot smoked, and this should be cleaned from racks and drip pan after each use.

A black, gummy residue will accumulate on some parts of your smoker and will impart a bitter taste to any food it touches. An occasional cleaning with warm water will prevent such accidents.

Another occasional cleaning chore is to remove some of the gummy deposits from the inside of the smoker. After a period of smoking, a dark brown residue will have coated some areas of the smoker. This concentrated mixture of water and smoke has a very bitter taste. It is not harmful for this to coat the walls of your smoker, but it is troublesome when meat comes in contact with the residue. It will pick up that same unpleasant taste. Therefore, be sure to keep these deposits from accumulating on food trays and hooks. Also, keep clean any other area which food might touch. Hot water alone is usually sufficient to remove this residue. Avoid the use of any cleaning agents. If their use is absolutely necessary to handle a stubborn deposit, rinse the area well with water after cleaning and burn a pan of wood fuel with no food in the smoker. This precaution will eliminate the possibility of harsh cleaning chemicals affecting the flavor of smoked food.

FUELS

The only strict rule applicable to the type of wood used to smoke food is that hardwoods are good and softwoods are bad. Hardwoods come from deciduous trees—those trees with broad leaves that shed every year. Softwoods are from trees with needlelike leaves. All softwoods—except tamarack, larch, and cypress—are evergreens.

Softwoods

Softwoods make poor fuel for smokers because they give off a strong-tasting mixture of pitch and resin that taints food and coats the inside of the smoker with a black, sticky film. This dark coating will also adhere to the food, interfering with both cooking and preserving. Common softwoods

Pine. include: cedar, cypress, fir, hemlock, larch, pine, spruce, tamarack.

Spruce.

Hardwoods

Hickory.

Cherry.

Of the more than one thousand separate species of trees in North America, most are hardwoods. Almost any hardwood will work fine in your smoker. Although much has been made of the term "hickory smoked," the best fuels are cut from fruit trees such as apple, cherry, or pear. Don't despair if you can't find these choice woods. Some hardwoods do indeed burn cleaner and sweeter than others, but you'll be hard pressed to detect a difference in, say, a whitefish that has been smoked with apple wood and another done with hickory. In other words, no matter which hardwood you use, the finished product will taste almost exactly the same. Some common hardwoods include: apple, ash, beech, birch,* butternut, cherry, cottonwood, chestnut, dogwood, elm, hickory, hornbeam, locust, mangrove, maple, oak, pear, sassafras, sweet bay, sycamore, thorn apple, tulip tree, walnut, willow.

Remember that you cannot always assume a tree is a hardwood just because its wood feels hard. Poplar, basswood, and even balsa are considered hardwoods in tree manuals, yet they're much softer than red pine and many other softwoods. When smoking, stay away from such light hardwoods as balsa and basswood because they burn too fast.

Corncobs

Corncobs make a perfectly acceptable smoker fuel. This does not mean you can use cobs discarded from a summer corn-on-the-cob meal. Use only well-dried and hardened cobs cut into small pieces for even burning. One bushel of cut cobs will last from thirty to forty hours in an electric smoker.

---

*Birch should be debarked because the bark emits tiny carbon and pitch particles when burned. These particles cling to whatever they come in contact with.

The most readily available forms of fuel: disks sawn from a tree limb; shavings from a wood plane; chips from an axe; corn cobs; sawdust or pulverized wood.

Wet Wood or Dry?

When smoking food, the object is smoke, not flame, so the wood need not be completely dried. Green or wet fuel is often preferred because the water aids smoke production while keeping the wood from bursting into flame.

Forms of Fuel

You can burn wood in the form of sawdust, shavings, chips, wafers, twigs, or chunks. Sawdust, shavings, and chips will prove the most convenient in an electric smoker, because their uniform size provides for easy storage and handling, and enables you to better determine the length of time a given amount of wood will burn.

You may eventually learn to calculate a regular burning time for a pan of sawdust or chips in your smoker. This can be a convenient method of figuring how much smoke to allot to a particular food. For example, perch fillets may acquire a pleasantly mild smoke flavor after one pan of sawdust; a good-size whitefish might need four pans.

A pan of sawdust for a portable electric smoker. This amount of fuel will last about forty-five minutes.

WHERE TO FIND WOOD

There are many places where you might find wood. They include: the makers of electric smokers; furniture or woodworking shops; sawmills; your own chips chopped with a hatchet; wafers cut from a branch with a bucksaw; wood shaved from old boards with a woodworking plane; and medium-size branches sawed into fist-size chunks. You might also look for old, abandoned orchards, blown-down trees, new construction areas, cuttings on power-line routes or any other source that may present itself.

CHAPTER III

EQUIPMENT
AND
MATERIALS

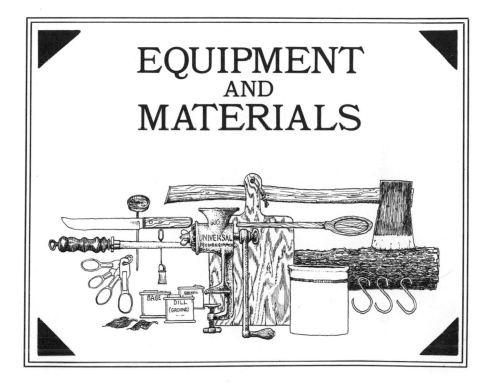

Every effort has been made throughout this book to keep equipment needs simple, to call only for those items that might be found in the average home. Most people will be able to begin full-scale smoking with but a minimal investment beyond the actual cost of building or buying their smoker.

Once you become a sophisticated, veteran food smoker, however, you may have the urge to buy better, more elaborate equipment. You will be wise to hold off on such purchases until you see exactly what your needs will be.

This section discusses the use of the various implements and materials mentioned in the book.

KNIVES

The most important tool needed to prepare food for your smoker is a sharp knife.

You'll need two: a heavy-duty butcher's model to cut and chop through fins, bones, and gristle, and a thin-bladed boning knife, with a four- or five-inch blade, for finer work. Forget about exotic Bowie types or Navy issues. They were great in the South Pacific, but they'll make a mess in your kitchen.

Sharpening

Few knives, even when new, are as sharp as they can or should be. The factory edge is often ground for all-around use, such as cutting cardboard, slicing vegetables, or hacking off green branches for weiner roasts. They're rarely honed razor sharp because the manufacturers know that most knives will encounter a variety of rugged tasks and that a very thin edge will nick or turn easily in such situations.

Putting a keen edge on a knife is a simple matter. Two aids are needed: a whetstone and a butcher's steel or smooth Arkansas stone.

You don't really need this many knives—one small one and one large one will suffice nicely—but make absolutely sure that however many you use, they stay sharp.

The ideal whetstone is a two-inch by eight-inch rectangular stone with coarse grit on one side and fine on the other. A smaller whetstone will work, but it should be set in a block of wood to keep it from sliding.

Stroke the blade across the rough side of the stone first, taking care to keep the knife edge at a constant 15° to 20° angle. The smaller the angle, the keener the final edge. Pretend you're slicing a thin piece from the stone.

Use some pressure. Always start at the blade's heel and draw it toward yourself, lifting the handle to sharpen the tip. Slicing away from your body might be safer, but it won't give as sharp an edge.

After a few minutes, flip the stone smooth side up and con-

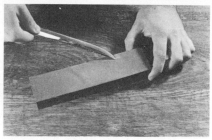

Proper sharpening technique on a whetstone: keep blade at a 15° to 20° angle to the stone.

tinue stroking, alternating blade sides at that same constant angle. When to stop? If the blade will catch or grab when lightly pulled over the face of your thumbnail, you're through with the whetstone.

Some experts encourage the use of oil with whetstones, a practice not actually necessary. Oil allows easier strokes and floats the steel filings, but that's about it.

Try to keep your whetstone clean. Once in a while brush the surface of the stone with turpentine to unclog any pores that might have been filled with dirt or metal filings.

Honing

The final honing may be accomplished with a smooth, marble-like Arkansas stone or a butcher's steel. These tools will remove little metal from your knife blade. Instead they'll sharpen the knife by smoothing out microscopic folds and creases on the edge just as a barber's leather strop aligns or smooths the edge of a straight razor.

The hard Arkansas stone is used as a sharpening whetstone, but a butcher's steel is easier to handle. It resembles a round, grooveless file and is made of Sheffield steel or ceramic. When

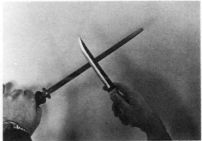

A few passes over a butcher's steel will renew the keen edge on your knife during big butchering jobs. The same 15° to 20° angle applies as with a whetstone.

faced with a long cutting session, such as cleaning a bucket of perch, a few quick strokes on the steel will replenish your knife's keen edge between fish.

If right-handed, hold the steel in your left hand, knife in right. Move knife downward, stroking lightly against the steel, with that same 15° to 20° angle as before. Alternate sides of the blade. A knife is considered razor sharp when the edge will shave dry hairs from your forearm, or smoothly slice through paper.

Care of Your Knives

Electric knife sharpeners and emory wheels are tricky to use. They remove metal too fast and their friction creates high temperatures that could easily ruin a blade's temper. Moreover, never wash good knives in a dishwasher. The high temperatures inside the machine may affect the blade's steel.

When storing your knives, don't let them rattle around in a utensil drawer; they'll get nicked and when fumbling for one, you may too. Instead, keep them in a flat cardboard box or on a magnetic device hanging on the wall.

CURING CONTAINERS

You'll need an assortment of nonmetallic containers for curing meat. Metal containers are no good because they react chemically with the salt in brine, imparting a bitter taste to the curing food.

If your curing job is small enough, you'll find a lot of good containers in your kitchen. Mixing bowls work well, as do casserole dishes, serving bowls, punch bowls, straight-sided jars, plastic containers of all sorts, and neglected crockpots.

Old-time earthenware crocks are the all-time favorite for brining and dry curing. Their size alone is enough to recommend them, not to mention their straight sides, which facilitate packing. They're also sturdy, easy to clean, and look attractive. They can still be found in many junk and antique stores at reasonable prices.

If you've got a whopper of a load to cure, you may have to use your bathtub. Take the time to clean and rinse it *thoroughly*. If the drain is not stainless steel, cover it so it won't be in contact with the brine. If you're in the habit of curing such loads, invest in an old tub, a stainless steel vat, or a wooden barrel.

THERMOMETERS

A thermometer, to measure the temperatures inside your smoker, is an essential piece of equipment. If you can't scare up

Smoke vents make excellent temperature checkpoints. The clothespin prevents the thermometer from completely blocking the vent. Although standard meat thermometers are only calibrated down to 140°F., they do measure lower temperatures.

an oven thermometer in your kitchen, run out to your local appliance store and get one.

Temperature is important in smoking food. Major heat distinctions are made between cold and hot smoking, but there are also finer gradations. Smoking temperatures are never precise, yet they may stipulate something like 100° to 120°F. There is no way of telling if you're anywhere near this range unless you have a thermometer.

The entire range of temperatures for smoking mentioned in this book is 70° to 225°F. Any thermometer that can record within this range will suffice. Actually, you could make do with a thermometer that only reads temperatures above 100°F., since for most cold smoking, it is sufficient to know that temperatures are below 100°F.

You'll get the most accurate readings if the thermometer is placed inside the smoker at about the level of the food. However, such an arrangement is awkward, since it means opening the smoker every time you want to check the temperature. Some meat thermometers measure a wide enough temperature range to be of value. They are ideal for gauging smoker temperatures because they can be inserted through a smoke vent with the temperature-sensitive tip inside and the gauge in full view.

Meat Thermometer

The use of a meat thermometer is the most reliable method of determining when hot-smoked food is cooked. If you plan to do much hot smoking, then this is another tool you should have.

Usually of stainless steel or aluminum, a meat thermometer is shaped like a spike with a large head. The pointed shaft is made to be pushed into the meat. The head is a thermometer gauge that registers the temperature at the tip of the shaft. The shaft must be inserted into the thickest part of the meat. To get an accurate reading, it is important that the tip not be in contact with bone or nestled in fat.

When working with roasts, use of the thermometer is no problem. For thinner cuts, the thermometer can be inserted horizontally or at any angle that will allow the tip to penetrate to the deepest part. With poultry, insert in the area of thickest meat on the breast.

As important as its telling when the meat is cooked, a meat thermometer can also indicate when the meat is *not* cooking. If smoker temperatures are not getting high enough to fully cook the meat, the internal temperature may increase extremely slowly. When it becomes obvious that the available smoker heat will not cook the meat in a reasonable amount of time, remove the meat and finish cooking it in an oven. If the meat is left for too long in a temperature range of 120° to 150°F., for instance, the heat will only dry the meat and not cook it properly.

CUTTING BOARD

There's no frustration as terrible as chasing a trout fillet over a slippery table or counter top, trying to cut it with a knife. Use

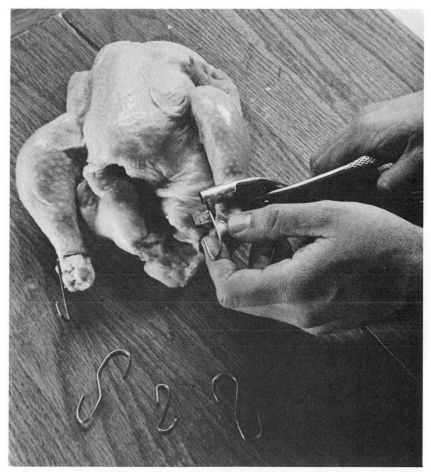

All sorts of makeshift hooks, for suspending meat in your smoker, can be made from a wire coat hanger.

a cutting board when preparing meat for your smoker. It saves wear and tear on counter tops and knives, and allows you to cut more efficiently.

BASTING BRUSH

Wild game and lean butcher meat will require basting while smoking. An inexpensive basting brush will come in handy.

WOODEN SPOON

Since brines can react with metal, you should not use metal spoons while curing. A wooden spoon will be needed to stir ingredients and rearrange curing meat.

HOOKS

Large cuts of meat, whole poultry, whole fish, and sausages are usually smoked while hanging from the top of the smoker. You'll probably find other uses as well for hooks of various shapes and sizes. You can have an endless supply of such items and it won't cost you a cent. Simply scavenge a few wire coat hangers, clip off an appropriate length with a wire cutter or pliers, and bend to shape.

Hangers come in several gauges. If the hook doesn't seem up to the task, try combining two or three of them. For heavy items, such as whole hams or shoulders, use a piece of string or twine to suspend them.

FROM THE PANTRY

Salt

Ordinary table salt will work satisfactorily in all the recipes and mixtures in this book, but it can be more expensive than other types of salt that can be purchased in larger quantities. Salt is packaged under a variety of names including Water Softener Salt, Rock Salt, Dairy Salt, among others. A fine-ground salt is best. Look for the designation "dairy fine" or "three quarters ground."

Since salt will come in varying consistencies, it is always given in a weight measure. If table salt is used, an approximate equivalent is one cup equals ten ounces.

Always use uniodized salt.

Sugar

The sugar called for in the recipes of this book is standard, commercial, granulated white sugar. It is given in both weight and quantity measures. Occasional recipes calling for the use of brown sugar will also give weight and quantity measures. The need for sugar in curing is basic, but the type of sugar is optional. Honey, molasses, maple syrup, or any other sweetener may be substituted in most of the recipes with fine results.

Herbs and Spices

Spices and seasoning play a prominent part in the preparation of food for smoking, as they do for any other preparation of tasty food. They serve to complement the smoke flavor as well as the natural flavor of the meat. If you have some favorite spices, by all means they should be incorporated into the recipes for cures, marinades, seasoned salt, etc.

Some of the recipes in this book may call for spices you seldom use. If you find a dust-covered box of such a spice hiding on the back of your shelf, do yourself a favor and throw it out. Spices lose their flavor after six months to a year. Increasing the amount called for won't help either. Get a fresh supply.

Some other hints: Dried herbs are much more concentrated than fresh; one teaspoon of a crushed, fresh herb equals about a quarter teaspoon of dried. When using leaves, crumple them into tiny pieces so the maximum amount of flavor is released. When trying out new spices in a recipe, go easy. To preserve flavor, keep herbs and spices from excessive heat and light.

Saltpeter

One ingredient—saltpeter—called for in many cures will be found in very few pantries. Saltpeter is potassium nitrate. Sometimes sodium nitrate, which has similar properties and is used in commercially cured products, is also called saltpeter.

Saltpeter is used in traditional curing formulas because it helps to preserve and color the meat. It is available in most drug stores, resembles sugar in appearance, and is sometimes labeled as "diuretic for animals."

Recently, both of these nitrates have come under suspicion from the U.S. Food and Drug Administration for their possible harmful effects. These chemicals turn into nitrites in the human body and may hinder the oxygen-carrying capabilities of the blood. Used as directed, however, these chemicals are currently considered safe.

Saltpeter is included in the recipes for curing foods in this book because most people have traditionally preferred the effect it has upon food. Its effect, however, is largely cosmetic. It creates a reddish coloration in meats, but the role it plays in preserving meat, is limited. If, therefore, you have reservations about using saltpeter, you sacrifice very little by omitting it from any curing recipe.

A substitute that is sometimes used for saltpeter is ascorbic acid (Vitamin C). It will produce as rosy a color in meats as will saltpeter. Used in its pure, crystalline form, it takes about a quarter teaspoon for every five pounds of meat. Substitute it in any of the following recipes in that proportion.

FOR SAUSAGE

Meat Grinder

If you plan to try your hand at making smoked sausage, you'll need a meat grinder. Elaborate, electrical grinders are on the market, some of which work as attachments to other appliances. If you're fortunate enough to have one of these, you are well prepared for sausage making. Hand-cranked models are more modestly priced, however, and will serve just as well.

Meat fed into a grinder is squeezed out through plates, or combs, with tiny holes. The size of the hole determines the consistency of the meat. A plate with ³⁄₁₆-inch holes can serve for sausage of a medium-coarse texture. Finer grained sausage will require two passages through the grinder, once with a ½- or ⅜-inch plate, then again with a ⅛-inch plate.

In a pinch, you can get by with only two plates—a fine ⅛-inch plate and a coarse plate, either ⅜ or ½ inch.

Muslin

You will also need something into which to stuff your ground meat. A simple sausage casing can be made of muslin cloth. Be sure to get unbleached muslin.

REFRIGERATOR

You can put fresh meat directly into your smoker and from there directly into your mouth, in which case the role of the refrigerator is minimal. In the vast majority of cases, however, you will definitely need room in the old fridge.

Unless you're going into smoking in a big way, there's no need to run out and buy yourself a second refrigerator. All that's needed is a little planning. Space is the problem. Arrangements must be made for the storage of meat beforehand, refrigeration during curing or marinating, and the storage of meat after smoking.

Since the proper preparation of smoked foods takes time and effort, most people like to smoke as much as possible on each occasion so they have some on hand for a while without the bother of preparing it for each meal. Obviously, refrigerator storage problems increase with the amount of meat you're smoking. There's nothing to storing a few pork chops, but a whole ham is another matter. Your smoking schedule will have to take into consideration available refrigerator space. Brine and marinating containers should be selected with refrigerator capacity in mind. Hooks may have to be rigged up to suspend sausages. You may choose to hard-cure when you have large quantities, simply because you can then get by without refrigerated storage.

During cold weather, it's a simple matter to store meat or curing containers outdoors or in a garage, as long as it is protected from snooping animals and below-zero temperatures. If you don't have the garage or the cold weather, give some thought to your refrigerator before smoking.

FREEZER

Most smoked food can be frozen with little or no loss of flavor. If you have a freezer, use it to advantage by smoking large quantities of meat. Aside from the cost of the meat, there is little additional expense in smoking a dozen pork chops as opposed to smoking only one. The savings in time and trouble is considerable. Smoked and frozen meat will always be as close as your freezer, ready for heating and serving.

Be sure to wrap all meats to be frozen securely. Wrap separately just the quantity needed for one meal. It's best to double-wrap all foods with good, moisture-proof freezer wrap to prevent drying and freezer burn. Label each wrapped package.

Meat that has been cured will not hold up as well under freezing as regular meat. Details on lengths of time for freezing smoked meat are given throughout the book.

RECORD KEEPING

A lot of experimentation will go into producing fine smoked foods. Unless you keep track of every smoking operation, you'll never know how to duplicate your most successful efforts. Record keeping is the answer to that problem. It's the only way to keep track of the myriad variables that contribute to the final flavor. A small tablet or notebook can be used for keeping your smoking record. It may seem like an unnecessary bother, but take the time to keep your record book up to date: it will eventually become your most valuable guide to smoking.

The major items contributing to final taste are listed below in **a sample record of one** smoking.

Smoking Record

Meat—Method of Preparation	*Fresh Whitefish hog dressed*
Method and Length of Cure	*3 hrs. in brine*
Ingredients of Cure Mix	*Basic brine mix. plus 2 T Allspice 6 bayleaves*
Additional Seasoning	*Rubbed with pepper before smoking*
Wood	*Cherry*
Smoking Time and Temperature	*3 hrs. at 140° – 150°*
Comments	*Too salty – good color and spicy taste – moist*

CHAPTER IV

CURES
AND
MARINADES

The art of smoking food is also the art of curing food. Food is only partially preserved by heat and smoke. To cure thoroughly and get a wide variety of flavor, appearance, and texture, salt and seasonings are equally important.

The effects of curing (salting) are several: (1) It reduces the moisture content of the meat; (2) It retards the formation of bacteria, thus delaying spoilage; (3) It adds flavor.

Curing is accomplished by packing meat in salt (dry curing) or soaking it in a concentrated salt solution (brining). In both methods, the salt dissolves into the meat while drawing out the moisture.

Old-fashioned methods usually called for lengthy periods of curing to prevent the meat from spoiling while in storage. Combined with long smoking over low heat to remove as much moisture as possible, meats could be preserved for several years. Of course, the end result was often a drier and tougher product than was desirable. The best example of what can be accomplished is the popular snack beef jerky, a meat that is thoroughly dried. Going to this extreme is hardly necessary today, when the preservative effects of the salt are often less important than the flavoring effects. Of course, even the small percentage of salt that results from a short curing time still serves to delay spoilage.

Spices and seasoning play a role in the smoking process not only for the extra flavor they provide, but also because they tenderize and color the finished product. Sugar, for instance, is used during curing to counteract the hardening effects of salt, which tends to dry meat. This gives rise to the expressions "sugar-cured" or "honey-cured," especially in reference to hams. Because of this quality, sugar is a basic ingredient in all brines and dry cures, whether it is in the form of white sugar, brown sugar, honey, molasses, or syrup. Each, of course, adds its own unique flavor.

Two nonflavoring ingredients frequently used in curing are monosodium glutamate, which serves to emphasize the flavor of other seasonings, and saltpeter (potassium nitrate). The coloring occurs as the saltpeter acts upon muscle fiber to produce denatured protein.

The use of seasoning is largely a matter of personal taste. Many spices can be used during or after the curing process to give an extra-tasty flavor to the meat. The following is a list of some of the spices and seasonings often used in cures:

allspice	garlic	onion powder
bay leaf	ginger	oregano
brown sugar	honey	paprika
celery salt	lemon juice	pepper
cinnamon	mace	sage
clove	maple syrup	soy sauce
dill	molasses	Tabasco sauce
dried mustard	nutmeg	white sugar

In the course of the cure, seasonings will become absorbed into the meat. Therefore, it follows that whatever flavor you wish to give your smoke products, you can. Obviously, some spices work best with certain meats, and different spices require varying amounts to impart the desired flavor. The list of spices and seasonings in the appendix will advise you in this regard.

The dry curing and brine recipes included in this chapter have proven reliable. They represent a good starting point for curing. Use them for a while. After you have gained experience and a feel for the curing process, begin to experiment with your own preferences.

A word of caution on experimentation: All experiments should first be conducted on a small scale. You may discover that your intuition about how a certain spice would affect a particular meat was all wrong. It will be much easier to accept this disappointment if you have only ruined, say, one small piece of salmon rather than an entire fish.

CURING

Both dry curing and brining are equally effective in preparing meat for smoking—few people are able to detect any difference in taste in the finished product. There are advantages and disadvantages, however, as far as length of time is concerned and the amount of attention each requires. Also, certain spices are more effective when used in brine. In later chapters, recommendations are given on which cures to use with certain meats.

The amount of time it takes to cure meat varies considerably. To a certain degree, curing time depends on how salty you like your meat. Fish fillets and thin slices of meat may acquire a pleasing salt taste after only one hour of cure. Hams, on the other hand, can require three to four days per pound. There is a difference between such thorough cures and curing that is done primarily for flavor. Most modern use of home smokers is intended to produce food that is not for long-term storage, in other words, meat that need not be protected against spoilage by high salt content. When preservation is not a consideration, curing time can be tailored exclusively to personal taste.

Meats at room temperatures will begin to spoil after only four to five hours. It is important, in any curing procedure that takes longer than this amount of time, to keep the meat chilled. Temperatures between 36° to 40°F. are ideal. Higher temperatures increase the chance of spoilage; lower temperatures slow salt penetration. The entire brine crock or container holding the dry-curing meat should be refrigerated if possible.

When curing, use ceramic, glass, plastic, or enameled containers, but never metal, which reacts with salt and may taint your meat.

BRINES

For the sake of taste and consistent quality, it is preferable to always mix brines of the same strength. An 80-percent salt solution makes a good brine. The brine mixtures given here are the amounts needed to make about two gallons of 80-percent brine. The exact amount of this strength brine produced by these mixtures will vary depending on water temperature, seasonings, and other factors.

The most accurate way of testing brine strength is with a salinometer, a graduated glass tube that floats in the brine, registering the strength of the solution by the level at which it floats. Since few homes have salinometers, a much simpler way of gauging brine strength is with a small, raw, unpeeled potato. Using the potato method, you can always make the right strength brine regardless of the quantity you need for curing.

In a container, put the amount of water you will need to cover

Any nonmetallic container can serve for brining or dry curing.

the meat to be cured. When you add the potato (it should be relatively fresh) it will sink to the bottom. Slowly begin to stir in the brine mixture. As the strength of the solution increases, the potato will become more buoyant. Eventually, when an approximate 80-percent solution is reached, the potato will float. You are then ready to begin brine-curing your meat.

The potato method will work equally well with a fresh egg.

Brine solutions that are too weak will not properly cure the meat and will also unduly increase its moisture content, thus requiring longer drying and smoking times. Brine solutions that are too strong may result in overly salty meat.

The primary advantage to making the same strength brine each time is consistency. If the brine produces meat with a higher salt content than you like, simply decrease the amount of time the meat cures in the brine. Do just the opposite if you prefer saltier meat.

Commercial smokehouses usually accelerate the curing process by pumping meat with brine. This is done with an instrument resembling a giant hypodermic needle. The brine is forced into the interior of the meat to hasten its curing effects. This technique is not recommended for the home smoker. For one, it frequently results in improper, or spot, cures; thorough curing takes time. If you don't want to wait for a "hard" cure, then do without it by following some of the shortcuts outlined in later chapters.

BRINING PROCEDURE

Once you have made a brine, completely submerge the meat to be cured in the liquid. Take care that none of the meat protrudes above the surface of the brine; meat that is exposed to the air will likely spoil. Weigh down the meat in some way so that there is no danger of it coming to the surface. An object such as a plate or water-filled jar can be placed inside the container, on top of the meat, to hold it down.

The contents of the brine container must be stirred occasionally. This is called overhauling. Use a wooden spoon to swirl the brine and gently rearrange the meat. This allows all surfaces to be fully exposed to the effects of the brine. If overhauling a large container of meat, pour off the brine, unpack, then repack the meat, stir the brine and return it to the container.

The length of time of a brine cure is dependent upon the type of meat and its size. See individual chapters for details.

BRINE RECIPES

Here are some of the brine mixtures you can try.

Basic Brine
3 pounds salt
1 pound (2 cups) sugar
1 tablespoon saltpeter
Use this basic brine first to see how it suits your taste, or try one of the following mixtures.

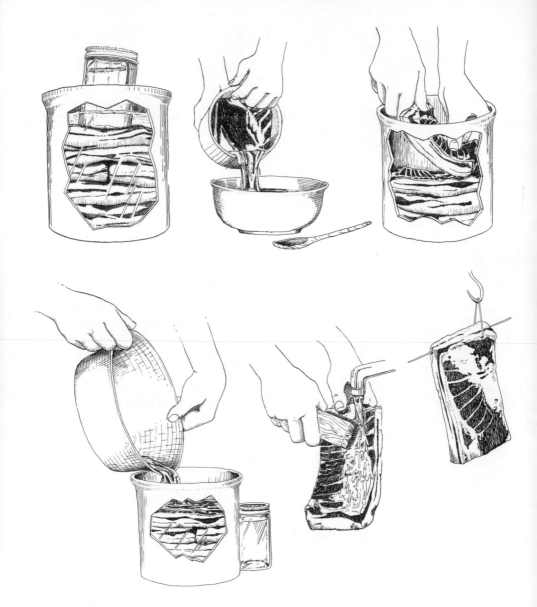

BRINE CURING: Pack meat in a crock and cover it with brine. A water-filled jar can act as a weight to keep the meat submerged. During lengthy cures, the contents must be overhauled; the first step is to pour off the brine. The meat is unpacked, then repacked in a new arrangement to assure uniform curing. After stirring the brine, to dissolve any ingredients that have settled out, return the same brine to the crock. Rinse and scrub the meat in fresh water to remove salt deposits. The meat must be allowed to dry before smoking.

Beef Brine
3 pounds salt
1 pound (2¼ cups) brown sugar
1 tablespoon saltpeter (optional)
2 tablespoons black pepper
5 crushed bay leaves
A more zesty beef brine is made by adding allspice, cloves, dill, oregano, or red pepper.

Fish Brine
3 pounds salt
1 pound (2¼ cups) brown sugar
1 tablespoon saltpeter (optional)
2 tablespoons onion powder
2 tablespoons oregano
Spice up your fish brine with allspice, crushed bay leaf, crushed clove, dried mustard, ginger, mace, nutmeg, or pepper.

Pork-Ham Brine
3 pounds salt
1 pound (2¼ cups) brown sugar
1 tablespoon saltpeter (optional)
2 tablespoons black pepper
6 crushed cloves
If you want a spicier cure, add allspice, cinnamon, or red pepper.

Poultry Brine
3 pounds salt
1½ pounds (3½ cups) brown sugar
1 tablespoon saltpeter (optional)
2 tablespoons dill salt
1 tablespoon onion powder
1 tablespoon sage
5 crushed cloves
Perk up poultry brine with ginger, mace, nutmeg, oregano, or paprika.

DRY CURES
In dry curing, a salt mixture is rubbed on all surfaces of the meat with special care being taken to poke some into and

around the bones. A thin layer of salt mixture is then patted onto the meat which is allowed to stand from several hours to several weeks in a nonmetallic container. As soon as the salt is applied, it will immediately begin to penetrate the meat. The moisture that is drawn out will make the surface of the meat wet.

For lengthy cures, only a portion of the appropriate amount of dry cure is used at first. After a period of time the cure is overhauled by unpacking the meat, resalting it with the remainder of the dry cure, then returning it to the container for the balance of the necessary time.

Specific dry-curing instructions for different meats are given later in the book, in their respective chapters.

DRY-CURE RECIPES

Here are several dry-cure mixtures. One pound of mixture is sufficient to cure about twelve to fifteen pounds of meat. Used on twelve pounds, it will provide a medium-to-strong cure. Used on fifteen pounds of meat, it will provide a milder salt flavor.

All mixtures should be blended thoroughly and, ideally, allowed to sit overnight.

Basic Dry Cure
2 pounds salt
¾ pound (1½ cups) sugar
1 tablespoon saltpeter
Most people prefer some variation of this basic formula to provide more seasoning.

Fish Dry Cure
2 pounds salt
¾ pound (1½ cups) sugar
1 tablespoon saltpeter (optional)
1 tablespoon black pepper
1 tablespoon oregano
1½ teaspoons onion powder
A spicy version of the above can be made by adding any of the following ingredients: allspice, crushed bay leaf, crushed clove, dried mustard, ginger, mace, or nutmeg.

Pork-Ham Dry Cure
2 pounds salt

1 pound (2¼ cups) brown sugar
1 tablespoon saltpeter (optional)
2 tablespoons black pepper
5 crushed cloves
3 crushed bay leaves
For a spicier mixture, add allspice, cinnamon, or red pepper.

PERSONALIZING YOUR CURES

Personalized cures can be made by using your own selection of spices and seasonings. Stick to the salt measure at first and experiment with varying amounts of sugar, according to preference. Begin adding spices in roughly the same amounts as those in the above mixtures, then increase or decrease the quantity as you see fit.

AFTER CURING

After curing, each piece of meat should be rinsed briefly in fresh water to remove salt, then set aside to dry. Where you encounter a stubborn encrustation of salt, it may be necessary to soak the meat for several minutes or even to scrub the surface with a stiff-bristled brush.

Meat may be patted with a paper towel to remove excess moisture. So that air can circulate freely around the meat, hang it on a line or lay it out on wire racks, not letting the individual pieces touch. If meat is not properly dried, there may be a sooty taste or a mushy texture in the finished product. One or two hours is usually enough time to dry small pieces exposed to the air. Very large pieces of meat may take up to twenty-four hours to dry thoroughly. When dry, a thin, clear, glossy coating of dissolved protein and nutrients will cover the surface of the meat. This signals that your meat is ready for smoking.

SEASONING BEFORE SMOKING

Many people like to season meat just prior to smoking. This can be done to flavor uncured meat or as a method of adding extra flavor to cured meat.

To flavor uncured meat, a dry-cured mix or a seasoned salt can be used. The salt and seasoning will impart a mild flavor to the meat as it smokes. If you don't want a salt flavor, just rub the surface of the meat with a blend of your favorite spices.

Even if you have cured your meat, you may wish to empha-

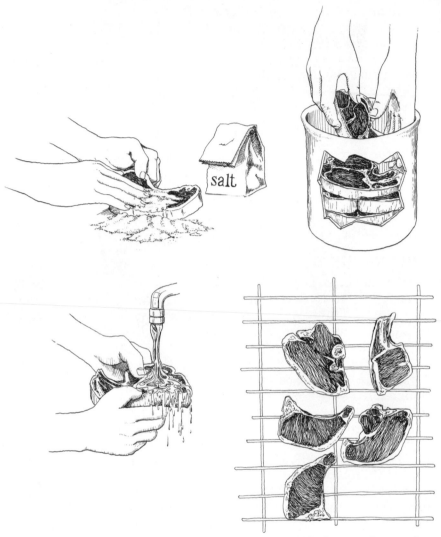

DRY CURING: Rub the meat with a dry-cure mix. Pack the meat in a curing container. After curing, rinse the meat under running water to remove the surface salt. Allow the meat to dry before smoking it.

Experiment to discover the seasonings that suit you best. Cure small pieces of meat with a variety of spices and see how they turn out. Be sure to keep a careful record so you can duplicate your successes.

size the flavor of a particular spice. Pepper can be sprinkled over the surface. Cloves can be stuck into the meat. Or the meat may be rubbed with whatever spice you choose.

SEASONED SALT

A well-seasoned salt will come in handy on many occasions. For meats to be smoked without a cure, rub one of the following mixtures onto the surface of the meat and let it add flavor during smoking. This versatile seasoning mix can also perform countless other quick-flavoring chores in the kitchen.

For best results, prepare this mix and allow it to sit for several days before using, so that the flavors can blend.

Seasoned Salt #1
1 cup table salt
4 tablespoons black pepper
4 tablespoons white pepper
4 tablespoons sugar
1 tablespoon monosodium glutamate
1 tablespoon celery salt
2 teaspoons onion powder
2 teaspoons garlic powder
1 teaspoon sage

Seasoned Salt #2
1 cup table salt
4 tablespoons sugar
2 tablespoons paprika
1 tablespoon monosodium glutamate
1½ teaspoons nutmeg
1½ teaspoons rosemary
1½ teaspoons marjoram
1 teaspoon ground cloves

SMOKED SALT

Smoke-flavored salt can work as a quick and tasty substitute for the real thing. To make up some for your kitchen, spread salt on a small tray or pan and place it in your smoker. Keep temperatures very low, around 70°F. Occasionally, stir salt so that it will all be exposed to the smoke. The salt will turn a light brown after about three to four hours, signaling it is done. Keep it handy in the kitchen to try on different foods.

MARINADES

Marinades can be used instead of cures to flavor and tenderize meat. They represent an excellent alternative for those who want to flavor meat without salt.

Most cookbooks contain marinade recipes listing dozens of different ingredients. Literally everything from soup to nuts has, at one time or another, been included as an ingredient in a marinade, but the basic ingredients are few and simple.

Acids, which work to tenderize the meat, are usually called for and can take the form of fruit juices, cider, vinegar, or wine. Lemon, orange, and pineapple are the most popular juices. Dry red wines, such as claret, or fortified wines such as Madeira, port, or sherry, are the best spirits to employ. White table wines are also good and are especially appropriate with white meat, where red wine would cause discoloration.

Oil is another frequently used ingredient. Vegetable oil, olive oil, or peanut oil is added to marinades to make meat more moist. It also aids the penetration of seasonings into the meat.

It may have occurred to you that the above sounds like the preparation of a salad dressing, and it very nearly is. Salad dressings often contain many of the same ingredients as a marinade. They are a convenient substitute when you are rushed.

Because of their acid content, marinades should only be used in nonmetal containers and, like brine, should only be stirred with a wooden spoon.

As in curing, the size of the cut of meat determines the length of marinating time. Chicken parts or small, stewing-size chunks of meat may acquire a light flavoring after only three to four hours. A roast of three to five pounds should soak twelve to twenty-four hours. It is difficult to be specific with time; different ingredients flavor at different rates, personal tastes vary, and tenderizing and flavoring requirements are often tailored to particular meats. The marinades provided here work well when used overnight. Eight to ten hours represents a reasonable period for most marinades. If in doubt, or if you usually prefer more subtle flavoring, cut that time in half.

When marinating, try to prepare enough liquid to cover the meat at least halfway, then once or twice during marination turn the meat over so that all its surfaces have a chance to soak.

The following marinade recipes should be considered as basic mixtures for their particular purpose. They will work perfectly well as given, but can also be used as a base to which you can add your own ingredients. Once you have tasted the effects of the various ingredients, improvise your own marinades. Keep in mind, however, that spices with strong flavors can easily overpower delicately flavored meats. Use such spices sparingly and avoid long marinating times.

Fatty Meat Marinade
¾ cup vinegar
½ cup lemon juice
½ cup orange juice
½ cup water

1 teaspoon onion powder
1 teaspoon pepper
Other ingredients to try—chopped celery, carrots, or parsley, garlic, lime juice, nutmeg, rosemary, sugar, or Tabasco sauce.

Fish Marinade

½ cup pineapple juice
4 tablespoons lemon juice
2 teaspoons soy sauce
¼ teaspoon pepper
1 clove garlic, crushed
Other ingredients to try—bay leaf, brown sugar, dill, ginger, olive oil, orange or pineapple juice, oregano, wine vinegar.

Small Game Marinade

2 cups water
1 cup wine
1 cup vinegar
½ cup vegetable oil
1 tablespoon oregano
1 medium onion, chopped
Other ingredients to try—bay leaf, garlic, nutmeg, marjoram, parsley, sage, or sugar.

Tough Meat Marinade

1 cup wine
1 cup water
½ cup vinegar
½ cup vegetable oil
2 teaspoons salt
1 teaspoon pepper
1 teaspoon onion powder
½ teaspoon garlic powder
Other ingredients to try—allspice, bay leaf, chopped carrots, celery, or parsley, fruit juices, or olive oil.

Venison Marinade

1 cup olive oil
1 cup vinegar
½ cup water

¼ cup parsley
1 tablespoon allspice
1 medium onion, chopped
Other ingredients to try—bay leaf, chopped carrots or celery, clove, garlic, mint, pepper, sage, thyme, or wine.

Very Lean Meat Marinade
1 cup wine
¾ cup vegetable oil
½ teaspoon salt
½ teaspoon pepper
¼ teaspoon garlic powder
Other ingredients to try—chopped carrots, celery, onion, or parsley, rosemary, savory, sugar, thyme.

Customize marinades by adding your favorite seasonings or those traditionally used with a particular meat. Spicier versions of the above recipes can be made by adding any of the following high-powered ingredients—allspice, cloves, cinnamon, dill, dried mustard, ginger, mace, oregano, paprika, red pepper, or Tabasco sauce.

OTHER USES
Marinades are versatile concoctions that serve well for basting meat while it is smoking or cooking. The marinade will have picked up the flavor of the meat after it has soaked; if the same marinade is then used as a baste, it will be richly laced with meat juices. This will make it especially tasty for use in gravies or sauces.

Another useful property of marinades is that they are effective at removing gamey odors from wild-animal meat. If you have soaked an earthy smelling piece of wild meat in marinade, it will probably be best to throw away the marinade rather than use it for other cooking chores, since the liquid will have picked up the unpleasant odor.

CHAPTER V

SMOKING
FISH
AND
SEAFOOD

If someone happened to mention "smoked fish" at a party, what would you think of? An expensive, imported two-ounce tin of smoked Atlantic salmon, sliced thin? Or perhaps a dish of kippered herring served in mustard sauce at a plush wedding buffet?

Well, salmon and herring stand back! because *any* edible saltwater or freshwater fish can be smoked into a delicacy fit for the finest occasion and for the most discriminating palate.

While some individuals swear that "oily" salmon, herring, and whitefish provide the ultimate in smoked eating, others prefer "drier" pike, or bass, or panfish; it's a matter of personal taste. There's no doubting, though, that smoking, in addition to lending an exotic zest to standard dinner fish, will also salvage species usually considered inedible. Such trash fish as suckers and carp can be rendered into delicious main courses, and Pacific salmon, even after spawning has occurred and their flesh begins to deteriorate, may still be successfully smoked.

You needn't be an expert fisherman (but it helps) to procure fish suitable for smoking. Fresh and frozen perch, rainbow trout, haddock, cod, and red snapper are available year round at your local supermarket, and clams, oysters, and shrimp also smoke with distinction.

FISH PREPARATION

Fish may be prepared in several different ways for curing and smoking. Of course, removal of the internal organs is always called for and should be accomplished as soon as possible. Small fish can be left whole if desired, with only their internal organs and gills removed.

Large fish will take quite a while to cure and smoke unless they are cut into smaller pieces. Dressing fish by any one of the following methods will greatly expedite the procedure and increase your chance of getting a thorough, uniform salt-and-smoke flavor.

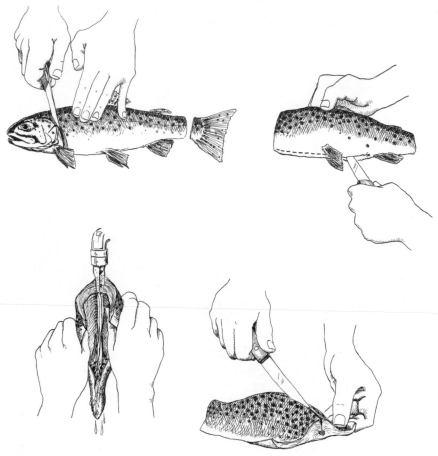

HOG DRESSING

Hog Dressing

Hog-dress fish weighing up to four pounds. Remove head and tail. Slit the belly and discard the entrails. Draw a knife gently along the top of the backbone, making a slight cut. Press on the fish to flatten it.

Fillet

Fillet fish weighing from four to ten pounds. Make a cut through meat to the backbone. Using the backbone as a guide, draw knife toward the tail, gently trimming each side of meat from bones with two separate cuts.

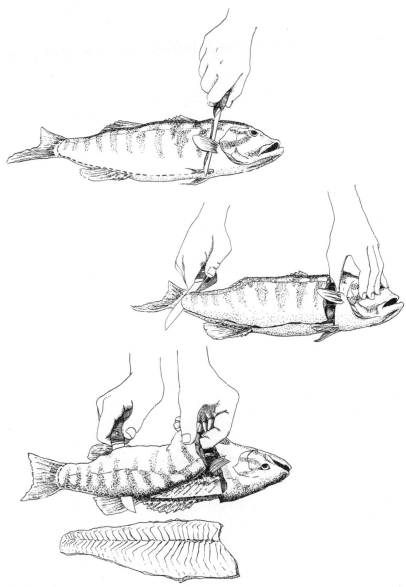

FILLETING

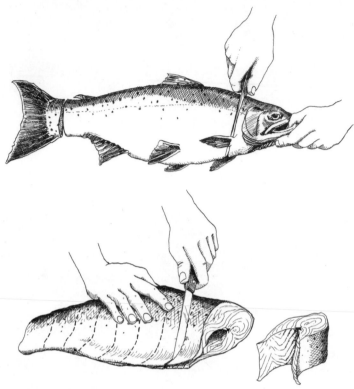

MAKING STEAKS.

Steak

Cut steak from large fish weighing more than ten pounds. Slice cleaned and gutted fish crosswise into steaks of uniform thickness.

When preparing fish, always cut the head off below the gills. Gills on a fish spoil rapidly, and if not discarded will taint adjacent meat. Fins may or may not be removed, but be sure to scrape the dark nerve materials from beneath the backbone.

Don't bother scaling small fish like perch or crappies because you won't eat the skin anyway. Larger fish, to be cut into steaks or filleted and sliced, should be scaled to allow easy cutting.

Never remove the skin. Skin helps reduce shrinkage and retains precious oils during the smoking process, assuring a moist and tender product.

Try to cut pieces of meat to a thickness no greater than one inch. Thicker pieces, or even large whole gutted fish, may be smoked, but the brine will take longer to work into the flesh, and the smoking time will have to be increased considerably.

Keep fish cool at all times; the flesh is tender and will soften if exposed to prolonged warm temperatures. When handling fresh or live fish, kill and clean as soon as possible, then rinse with cold running water, pat dry, and refrigerate.

Shelled seafoods, such as clams, oysters, and shrimp, acquire unique flavors when smoked. They may be prepared by lightly steaming or boiling. Remove clams and oysters from their shells and peel shrimp before curing and smoking.

BRINE CURING

Prepare a brine solution and follow the brining procedure outlined in Chapter IV. If you have prepared your fish as suggested earlier, they will require a brine cure of one to four hours. For one-inch-thick pieces, two or three hours should provide a medium cure. More or less time will raise or lower the salt content of the finished product. Very thin fillets may require as little as thirty minutes in brine to give them a mild cure. For curing larger, thicker pieces of fish, six to ten hours represents the range for a light-to-heavy cure.

Clams, oysters, and shrimp all require about thirty minutes brining.

DRY CURING

Quick Dry Cure

If you're especially eager to taste your fish, or simply don't have the time to wait for a brine cure, here's a faster way. The thinner the piece of fish, the more effective this method of curing.

After the fish has been properly prepared, a dry-cure mixture (see Chapter IV) is gently rubbed over the entire surface. Care must be taken with delicate varieties that the flesh is not bruised or torn. Pat the mixture around bones where salt penetration is often most difficult. Lay the fish out on the racks of the smoker and begin smoking at a temperature from 150°F. to 170°F. After about thirty to forty-five minutes, a thick white liquid will have oozed from the surface of the meat. This is moisture being drawn out by the salt and heat. It contains dissolved salt and protein matter. It should be removed at this

The quick dry cure. Fillets are merely sprinkled with seasoned salt or dry-cure mix before smoking.

point with a basting brush so you can resalt the fish. Resalt by sprinkling with more of the dry-cure mixture, then continue smoking for an additional thirty to forty-five minutes, or until the fish turns a golden brown and flakes when it is pressed with a fork.

Standard Dry Cure

A standard dry cure can be accomplished by lightly rubbing dry-cure mixture onto the fish. Pat the mixture on the flesh so that a thin layer remains, then refrigerate the fish and allow it to cure for five to eight hours, depending on thickness and desired salt content.

DRYING

After either method of curing, fish should be lightly rinsed in cold water and allowed to dry thoroughly before being smoked.

SMOKING

Cook, then Smoke

Fish may be taken right from the oven and placed in the smoker. Most fish will acquire a good smoke flavor in this manner after about two hours. Smoke at temperatures of 100° to 120°F. The meat will turn a golden brown and will taste great.

If salt flavor is desired, fish may be cured prior to cooking, then smoked for flavor.

Cold Smoking

If a mild smoke flavor is all you're after to liven up a favorite dish, use a brief period of cold smoking. One to four hours offers a mild-to-strong flavor that will hold up under cooking. Keep smoker temperatures low—around 70° to 90°F.

Hot Smoking

Lightly grease or oil the racks of the smoker to avoid sticking. Arrange the pieces of fish evenly on the racks, taking care none of them touch each other. Fillets should be placed skin side down.

As with curing, there are too many variables to be able to give exact times for smoking. A temperature between 150° and 170°F. will thoroughly cook and smoke a thin fillet within one hour. One-inch steaks might take six to eight hours.

It's best to check the fish periodically. Some lean fish dry out rapidly and may require basting. Brushing them with cooking oil, butter, or margarine will keep them moist. If you baste fish while using the quick dry cure, resalt them before further smoking.

When fish are done, they will be a pleasing golden brown. Large pieces, however, sometimes might appear done on the outside, but actually have not been thoroughly cooked. To test, simply press at the flesh with a fork. When it flakes apart under pressure, it's done.

Depending on how dry you want the finished fish, it can remain in the smoker even after it's been fully cooked to allow more moisture to escape.

SALMON

Because of the excellent quality of smoked salmon, it is worth lavishing a bit more attention on the preparation of this fish.

To help retain the fresh flavor of this delicate meat, especially if it is to be stored for a while before smoking, be sure to remove the fat strip along the top (dorsal) fin line, and also the belly flap from each side, including the bottom fins.

A simple, yet reliable brine can be made from the following:

Smoked salmon—a gourmet delight from any smoker, especially your own.

1½ pounds salt
½ pound (1⅛ cups) brown sugar
1 teaspoon onion powder
4 bay leaves, crushed
Allow thick salmon steaks to brine-cure for eight hours.
Wash and let dry.

Hot-smoke at about 170°F. until flesh is flaky. At this point the meat will be moist. Many people prefer their salmon on the dry side. Allowing the fish to remain in the smoker for one or two additional hours will dry the meat more.

Salmon tastes best with a strong smoke flavor. Although it can be cold-smoked for a brief time to acquire a light flavor, and then included in some recipe, you'll be missing out on the fish's full taste potential. If you don't want to cook the salmon fully in your smoker because you have some exciting recipe waiting that calls for raw fish, then cold smoking is fine, but give the fish plenty of time to flavor. A minimum of four hours is necessary to bring out the best in salmon.

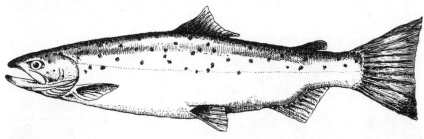

Atlantic salmon.

CARP

Many so called trash fish can be smoked into culinary masterpieces. Only in the United States are carp considered lowly; in Europe and Asia these large-scaled fish are highly sought, and even raised as game and food fish.

The larger the carp, the better. Fillet it and cut into chunks or, if it is exceedingly large, hog dress it and cut it into steaks. Proceed with one of the brining and smoking instructions described in this chapter and you'll be hard pressed, when it's finished, to taste the difference from salmon or trout.

SUCKERS

Suckers have been relatively unpopular due to their bony

makeup—it's too hard to obtain the meat because of the abundance of small bones. As a consequence, most fishermen don't even give them a nod.

The truth is that sucker meat is sweet and delicious and can be smoked very successfully. Just hog dress and skin a sucker, then poach or boil it until the meat can be gleaned from the bones. Refrigerate the meat, then form into fish cakes, which can be fried, then smoked.

CLAMS, OYSTERS, AND SHRIMP

After being lightly cooked and thoroughly dried, lay any of these seafood tidbits out on the oiled racks of your smoker. (Since smoker racks are often too widely spaced to hold such small items, place a piece of metal window screen over them so the seafood won't fall through.)

Start with the smoker cold and slowly build up the heat. This amounts to a period of cold smoking when the moisture will be drawn out. About fifteen to thirty minutes of smoking in the 120° to 150°F. range should be sufficient for a pleasing smoke flavor.

These hot-smoked shrimp go right from the smoking rack to the hors d'oeuvre plate.

CRAWFISH

Drop live crawfish into boiling water and cook until the shells turn red. Open the shells and remove the meat. Sprinkle a little dry cure over meat, or brine for a half hour, smoke forty-five minutes to one hour for a terrific hors d'oeuvre.

FROG LEGS

Starting with a whole frog, sever the hind legs as if cutting the V from a Y, then pull the skin and membranes off with needlenose pliers.

Soak the legs for several hours in fish brine, then smoke at about 140° to 150°F. for one to two hours. The meat will possess a delicate flavor and consistency much like that of chicken. It is delicious hot or cold. Feature the meat in a stew or chowder, or serve whole legs as a garnish to a seafood platter. Or why not try a frog-leg cocktail?

SNAPPING TURTLE

Many other aquatic turtles are edible, but snappers are by far the best. Remove shells by separating the top from the bottom half. Cut out the meat and discard all the yellow fat. Slice the meat into serving-size pieces and wash first in salt water with a dash of vinegar added, then in clean water. Brine overnight, then smoke for one to three hours at 140° to 150°F. Finish off large chunks in the oven.

EEL

Nail an eel by its head to a wooden post or stud. With a very sharp knife, cut all around the neck, then grasp the slippery covering with a needlenose pliers and forcefully pull down, striping off the skin. Discard entrails and cut the meat into bite-size sections. Wash and soak in brine overnight. Smoke as you would snapping turtle.

STORAGE

Well-cured and smoked fish should still be stored under refrigeration, where they will last a minimum of three weeks.

Freezing does not impair the flavor of smoked fish. Wrapped well—or better, double wrapped—smoked fish will last almost indefinitely, to be enjoyed at any time in the future. After thawing, eat cold or reheat in oven or broiler.

CHAPTER VI

SMOKING
BUTCHER
MEAT

Beef
Pork
&
Lamb

J ust because your favorite grocer fails to keep Southern-cured hams or country-style bacon in stock, that certainly doesn't mean you have to drift through life without ever enjoying the unique flavors offered by smoked meats. Not when any cut of meat can be successfully smoked, and you, yourself, can smoke them all!

Of course, there is no set way to smoke all meats; while some lend themselves to traditional curing-smoking methods, some are best cured but not smoked, and others may be cooked first and then smoked. It depends on the meat, your personal taste, and the amount of time you're willing to invest toward the final product.

Let's say you've purchased a fresh cut of beef from your butcher. Depending on the cut, you can follow any one of a number of processing paths. Your first option is to cure or not to cure.

TO CURE OR NOT TO CURE

The purpose of curing is to impart flavor and to preserve. If you plan to eat your smoked meat within a few days, or if you plan to freeze it, then curing is not necessary as a preservative measure. Most people, however, would not dream of smoking meat without curing it in some way because the smoky taste they have come to appreciate is often strongly influenced by the salt and seasoning of the cure.

Some of the smoking procedures in this section do not include curing for one reason or another. To an extent, the curing decision depends on the type of meat and the method chosen for its preparation. It is generally held, for instance, that a heavy salt cure is more compatible with pork than with beef. Some short-cut methods of preparation may even eliminate curing as a time-saving factor.

Recommendations on curing, or not curing, are given throughout the text. The final decisions on this, as on all other matters of individual taste, are yours.

COLD SMOKING FOR FLAVOR

After you've decided on the cure you must select either hot or cold smoking.

Cold smoking can be used simply to flavor meat. A period of cold smoking at temperatures below 120°F. for one half to four hours will likely add the degree of smoke flavor you want. It can work wonders in enhancing the taste of leftovers or lower-grade cuts of meat. Hamburgers and hot dogs, for example, can be placed on the smoker's food racks and smoked for an hour to turn them into special treats. Strips of meat from a previous night's pot roast can be given new life with a little smoke.

Remember, whenever you add smoke flavor to meats that are to be cooked later, smoker temperatures of 70° to 90°F. are adequate, and this range also applies to the larger, high-quality meats. Chops, steaks, and roasts can be flavored in this manner and then cooked in the oven or broiler. Smoke chops and steaks one to four hours for a mild to strong flavor. Roasts may take up to six hours.

If desired a seasoned salt, or a dry-cure mixture, may be rubbed over the meat just prior to smoking to provide extra flavor.

Many people prefer to cook meat before, rather than after, smoking. They claim that the cook-smoke method offers a better smoked flavor because none of the smoke taste is lost in the cooking process.

Another factor that should be taken into consideration in choosing between cook-smoke and smoke-cook is that smoking reduces the moisture content of meat. For moist or fatty meats this is no problem. But cooking first and then smoking might adversely affect dry cuts. Baking a lean beef roast and then submitting it to prolonged smoking may remove too much moisture. Dry meats should be smoked first, and then cooked, if necessary; you'll have much better control over the finished product. If you don't have a choice, and the meat has already been cooked, you can counter the drying effect by using low temperatures and basting during the smoking periods.

Smoking times for the cook-smoke method are usually one to four hours.

HOT SMOKING TO FLAVOR AND COOK

Any temperature of 100°F. or higher cooks meat. Naturally, the greater the heat, the faster the cooking. The terms hot smoking and smoke cooking refer to any smoking process that employs temperatures above 120°F.

Hot smoking is a great time saver and will allow you to produce a ready-to-eat product entirely with your smoker. This contrasts with cold smoking, where meat must be partially cooked outside the smoker, usually in an oven.

Smoking times and temperatures will vary with the kinds of meat, the thickness of the cuts, and the amount of doneness you require. Temperatures in excess of 200°F. are most convenient, but lower heat, around 170°F. is sufficient to smoke-cook most meats if the smoking period is appropriately lengthened. True, these temperatures seem low in comparison with those used in a kitchen oven, but they are hot enough to cook most meat properly. And longer cooking times at lower temperatures often result in meat that is more moist than an identical cut cooked in a traditional fashion.

A meat thermometer should be used to gauge when large cuts are cooked. The actual determination as to whether small cuts are done can be made by inspection.

COLD SMOKE—HOT SMOKE

With hot smoking, some meats, especially the thinner cuts, may become thoroughly cooked before they have been in the smoker long enough to acquire the degree of smoke flavoring you want. The larger cuts will usually remain in the smoker long enough to absorb a sufficiently zesty smoke flavor.

To add more smoke flavor to the thinner cuts, a period of cold smoking may be used prior to hot smoking. Again, it's a matter of personal taste. Determine about how long it will take for a particular cut of meat to cook while hot smoking. If experience has indicated that you prefer a stronger smoked flavor in the resulting product, then cold smoke first.

PORK

No meat is more improved by smoking than pork. Ham, bacon, chops, indeed everything that comes off a pig lends itself to smoking. Although some of these cuts are available in stores already smoked, you'll discover a vast difference between smoked items you buy and those you make. Commercial products come in a poor second.

But before you try to smoke any pork, heed this warning: Trichinosis is a disease transmitted through infected pork and precautions are necessary to prevent occasional infected meat from ending up on your dinner table. Any of the following conditions will destroy trichinae worms:

Freezing at −20°F. for six to twelve days.

Freezing at −10°F. for ten to twenty days.

Freezing at 5°F. or lower for twenty to thirty days.

Heating of meat to 137°F. throughout.

Curing and smoking alone are not sufficient to remove all danger of infected meat. Smoke-cooking of pork is possible in those smokers capable of sustaining high enough temperatures. However, because of the necessity to have pork thoroughly cooked before eating, it is usually cooked in the kitchen either before or after smoking.

As stated before, any cut of pork can be cured and smoked; those you can handle will be limited only by the size of your smoker. Some whole hams or shoulders will be too large to accommodate. In that case, excellent results can still be achieved by slicing the larger cuts into pieces. By working with ham and pork cuts that do not exceed an inch to an inch and a half in thickness, your curing and smoking times can be shortened considerably. And, since thorough processing of large cuts can sometimes take as long as a month, shortcuts are desirable and often necessary.

Old-time hard-cure methods were used primarily to preserve meats for long-term storage when refrigeration was unavailable. Unless preservation is your main purpose for smoking, there's no big advantage in preparing meats the long way.

The following sections outline several methods of smoking pork, from quick and easy procedures that can add flavor just before mealtime, to thoroughly detailed instructions for hard-curing whole hams.

Cook, then Smoke

A short period of cold smoking at 100° to 120°F. for pork that has already been cooked is the fastest way to get a mouth-watering flavor. This handy method will produce a moist, smoked meat without the salty taste from curing.

Take all the usual precautions and cook the pork before smoking. Ideally, take the meat directly from the oven and place it on the smoker racks. Slide a shallow tray beneath the meat to catch drippings. Never let grease drip onto the heating element or the smoke baffle—a fire could result.

Incidentally, the smoker drippings will also carry the smoke flavor, and you might want to add a little to your gravy mix.

Pork prepared in this way may be eaten straight from the smoker, refrigerated for several days before use, or stored in the freezer.

For chops, ham slices, and spareribs, cook pieces that are no thicker than one inch, then smoke forty-five minutes to one hour. Roasts three to four pounds will need to smoke about forty-five minutes to one and a half hours, and larger roasts will require three to four hours in the smoker for adequate flavoring.

Try giving your store-bought bacon an old-time flavor with additional smoking. About half an hour for strips and up to three hours for small slabs.

Curing and Smoking Small Cuts

Most of the pork you smoke will probably be small cuts purchased from a supermarket or butcher shop. Thin slices of pork roast, ham slices, individual chops, and spareribs can all be processed within a reasonable amount of time.

To cure these cuts, rub them with curing mixture, then pat an additional thin layer over the surface, place in a curing container and refrigerate six to ten hours or overnight. If you elect to use a brine instead of a dry cure, it will take slightly longer to achieve the same strength cure. Mix brine from recipes in Chapter IV and cure for seven to twelve hours. Exact length of cure depends on the thickness of the meat and the desired strength of the salt taste. It's always best to start out with the least amount of brining time on your first try, then adjust to longer or shorter times to fit your tastes.

After removing meat from the brine, wash the salt from the surface and dry the meat before smoking.

Ideally, the temperature during smoking should be held between 100° and 120°F., a heat just hot enough to melt the surface fat. Smoke one to four hours for a mild-to-strong smoke flavor.

Small cuts may be cooked immediately after smoking; if not, they should be eaten within a reasonable period of time.

The large cuts of pork packed in a curing container (left) are about to be covered with brine. While being cured in the brine, the meat must be weighed down to keep it submerged (right).

Curing and Smoking Large Cuts

Naturally salt will take longer to thoroughly penetrate large cuts of pork, so the curing process that took ten hours for your chops will take about ten days for your roast. Rushing this curing time will result in improperly cured meat in which the salt flavor will not be uniform throughout.

Determine the correct amount of dry-cure mix for the weight of meat to be smoked. Rub 50 to 60 percent of that amount onto the meat then pack in a curing container. Halfway through the curing time, resalt the meat with the remaining mixture.

Cure cuts of one to four pounds for seven to eight days. Larger roasts or hams up to twelve pounds will take ten days to cure. Add two to four days if brine curing. Overhaul by stirring brine and rearranging meat several times during cure. Dry-curing meat should also be turned over or rearranged in its container during the cure to allow the salt to penetrate uniformly. Meat should always be refrigerated throughout cure. Wash off the salt and let the cuts dry before smoking.

For a tasty flavor variation, rub the pork with seasonings just before smoking. Black pepper adds its famous tartness, and seasoning salts work well. You might want to test your own concoction of spices. (Remember the note on experimentation in Chapter IV.)

Here are a few basic guidelines:

Slab Bacon—If you're ordering a custom slab of bacon from a butcher, ask for the brisket end with the skin removed. Consider also the size of your smoker when ordering the cut. Smoke two to four hours.

Butt—The butt end of the loin will usually weigh about three pounds. Smoke it for two to three hours.

Boneless Loin (Canadian Bacon)—A whole boneless loin will average five to six pounds and cost almost as much as a trip to Europe. It can be cured and smoked in one piece, or cut in half across the grain. Smoke four to five hours for a real treat.

Whole Ham—To avoid a curing time longer than ten days, remove, or ask the butcher to remove, the long bone from the ham. This will allow you to reach all inside surfaces with the cure and speed things along. Smoke four to five hours, until the meat turns a rich, reddish brown.

Hard-Curing Pork

Sometimes called "Country-Style Smoked," meat prepared with this method can be stored for long stretches of time without refrigeration. Such prolonged storage can be a problem, however, if proper procedures are not followed. Old-time instructions called for a hard-cured ham to be buried in a cool, dark, and dry grain bin. Meat that is not kept cool enough will turn rancid. Too much moisture in the air will encourage mold growth. (An air-tight wrapping used for unrefrigerated storage is discussed later.)

Two basic qualities of hard-cured pork are strong salt flavor and strong smoke flavor. After a piece of meat has been smoked, not much can be done about the smoke flavor. It's there for good. It could be masked or hidden with seasonings, but generally it's an irreversible process. Not so with salt taste. If you find that a particular cut of meat has been brined for too long, simply soak the piece in water for a while. As the curing and smoking process adds salt and reduces the water content, so soaking will return moisture to the meat and reduce the salt concentration.

Bacon, loin, ham, and shoulder are the cuts of pork that are often hard cured. Bacon, in this section, means slab bacon, not the prepackaged, presliced commodity you find at the supermarket. Slabs can be purchased from any butcher or butcher counter at a grocery store. They weigh somewhere around eight pounds for a medium-size slab. If you own a portable, electric smoker, remove the racks and hang cured slabs on the hook at the top of the smoker. Any cut that can be suspended without touching the sides or bottom can be smoked.

Curing

To prevent spoilage, begin with chilled meat and keep it refrigerated throughout the curing process. For hams and shoulders, use one pound of dry cure for twelve pounds of meat. Use half that amount for bacon. In other words, half a pound of cure for twelve pounds of bacon. The dry-cure mix used on bacon may be applied all at once. For hams and shoulders, approximately half the mixture should be used at the start, and the rest saved for resalting when the cure is overhauled.

Most of these cuts are not of uniform thickness, so apply cure

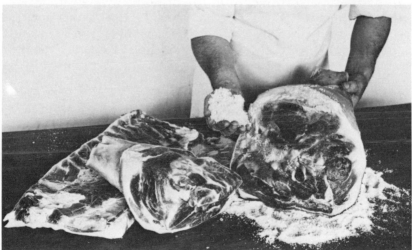

When dry-curing large cuts, such as those shown on the opposite page, rub curing mixture on all the surfaces of the meat. The heavier the cut, the more mixture you should apply. After applying the dry cure, pack the meat away in a barrel or large crock. The cuts will have to be resalted after the first six to eight days. Simply remove the meat from the curing container, rub on the rest of the dry-cure mix, then repack the meat for the rest of the curing time.

with a heavy hand to the heftier areas, patting it so that it adheres. Poke the mixture into the joints and all around bones. Cover the lean face of hams with a ⅛-inch layer, and the other surface areas with a thinner but complete coating. Carefully set meat into the curing container so none of the cure falls off.

Curing time is determined by the weight of the cut, but minimum times apply. Bacon and loins require one and a half days per pound, hams and shoulders two days per pound. Twenty-five days is the minimum for any cut thicker than two inches. Slabs of bacon under ten pounds should be cured for at least fifteen days. Resalt large cuts after the first week.

If brine curing, simply stack meat in container, weigh it down to keep it submerged, then cover with brine. Allow fifteen to twenty days in brine for bacon and loin pieces. The thicker they are, the more time is needed to cure them. Brining time for hams and shoulders is figured at three and a half to four days per pound, with a twenty-eight-day maximum.

Brine curing meat will require your attention at least once a week. To overhaul, remove meat from container, pour off brine, repack meat, then stir the brine and pour it back. This is necessary to rearrange meat for uniform exposure and to keep the ingredients from settling out of the brine.

If the brine turns sour or thickens to the consistency of syrup—throw it out. Save the meat by scrubbing it in hot water. Thoroughly clean the curing container, then repack the meat in new brine with a lower salt content. This ordeal can usually be avoided if the container is kept refrigerated.

Smoking Hard-Cured Pork

After curing, remove excess salt by soaking meat in cold water for fifteen minutes, or the meat can be scrubbed under running water with a stiff brush to remove stubborn encrustations of salt. Allow the meat to dry completely. This may take overnight or longer.

Smoke pork at 100° to 120°F. for a minimum of twenty-four hours; forty-eight hours is better. Twice that is not too long. Obviously, you can't be by your smoker all that time to see that things go right. Don't worry. The hours of smoking need not be continuous hours. It's no problem if the fire goes out overnight; just make allowance for the amount of time the meat was without smoke and continue smoking.

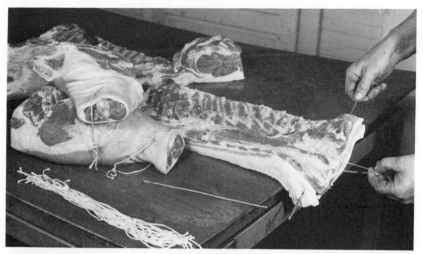

Hang large cuts of pork by a sturdy piece of twine. To prevent the twine from tearing through bacon slabs, use a skewer, as shown here.

LONG STORAGE OF HARD-CURED PORK

Hard-cured pork must be protected from insects, light, air, and moisture. To do this, it must be covered with a sturdy wrapping. If each individual piece of meat is wrapped, bagged, and hung separately, it can be stored safely in a dark, cool, dry, well-ventilated place.

After smoked meat has cooled, wrap each piece carefully in several layers of waxed paper, then sew it in a muslin bag. The layers of waxed paper must be thick enough to keep grease from soaking through to the bag. The meat can be protected further from mold and vermin by painting it with a hard, outside coating. Lime, clay, or flour can be mixed with water to a pasty consistency, then painted on to form a protective crust.

Hard-cured meat can be frozen without harming its flavor. Whole hams will keep for up to a year in the freezer. Entire cuts of meat can be wrapped separately and frozen or more convenient slices can be wrapped for individual meals.

Don't despair if your meat develops surface mold. This does not affect its wholesomeness. Scrub or cut away mold and rub the meat with cooking oil to delay future mold growth.

Smoke Cooking Pork

The cold-smoking procedures outlined in this section serve

only to flavor and help preserve meat. Pork can be safely smoke-cooked in a smoker by holding temperatures at 200° to 225°F. until a thermometer in the thickest portion of the meat registers a temperature of 170°F. If your smoker is capable of reaching higher temperatures, 250°F. for instance, better yet—your meat will be cooked that much sooner. Smoke-cooked pork is ready to eat.

BEEF

Dried beef, corned beef, pastrami—these and other cured and smoked beef products are readily available in the supermarket. If you want them from the store, it'll cost you an arm and a leg. If you want to make them yourself, all you need is a little time.

Like pork, the curing and smoking of beef can be handled in a wide variety of ways.

Cook, then Smoke

Although this procedure is usually reserved for roasts, any cut of beef that has previously been cooked can be cold-smoked for a rich, smoked flavor—even ground beef.

The procedure is the same as with pork. Smoking time is from one half to four hours, depending on the thickness of the meat and the desired flavor.

Curing Beef

If you're working with an inexpensive cut of beef, use a cure. It can make a dramatic improvement in flavor and taste. But curing should by no means be reserved only for low-grade beef. Good cuts can be made even better by curing and smoking. The high quality of the meat and the distinct flavoring of the cure-smoke will combine for an extraordinary taste.

This section includes directions for giving a traditional cure to beef. If meat is not for storage, curing time may be tailored to suit your taste.

Ribs: Cure beef ribs in a standard 80-percent brine or in a dry cure for one to four days. Rinse with water after curing and allow to dry completely, then cold smoke at 70° to 90°F. for one to four hours. Ribs can be removed at this point to be barbequed or included in your favorite recipe, or they can be completely cooked by hot smoking. Hot smoke at 200° to 225°F. until they are done—when bones break away from the meat.

Steaks: A one- to two-day cure will provide sufficient salt

flavor for most steaks. Especially thin steaks may take as little as twelve hours. If your palate revolts at curing choice steaks, skip the cure and go right to the smoking. One hour of cold smoking will provide a mild smoke flavor. Continue smoking up to four hours for a strong flavor.

Steaks can be cooked quickly at smoker temperatures over 200°F. Gauge for yourself when meat is done as you like it. Remember that smoked beef, especially if it has been cured, will appear more red than ordinary cooked beef.

Roasts: Curing roasts will require about two days per pound. Lengthen or shorten this time if the cuts are unusually thick or thin. Either a brine or a dry cure may be used. For cures that take over a week, resalt on the fifth day. Overhaul cure every three or four days to ensure uniform salt penetration.

Wash all meat after curing and allow to dry. Be sure to allot plenty of time for the surface of the meat to dry. You can expedite things somewhat by patting the meat with a paper towel after washing. Thorough drying can take twelve to twenty-four hours.

Smoking Beef

If you're hot smoking, insert a meat thermometer into the thickest part of the roast, avoiding the bone, and smoke at 200° to 225°F. until the internal temperature of the meat indicates that it is done to your satisfaction—140°F. for rare, 160°F. for medium-rare, 170°F. for well done. A meat thermometer can be inserted horizontally into steaks or small roasts for accurate cooking.

Hot smoking will provide a mild smoke flavor. To strengthen smoke taste, begin with one or two hours of cold smoking.

Smoke-cooking times are not nearly as precise as oven-cooking times. To assure meat is done as you like it, use a meat thermometer whenever possible.

Corned Beef

Corned beef is simply beef that has been hard cured. Commercially packaged, it is often made of the poorer or fattier cuts. The curing methods described for roasts actually produce corned beef, although longer cures of three to four days per pound are usually called for. Smoke as you would a beef roast. Instead of smoke cooking, however, cold smoke for flavor, then cook as you would a regular corned beef.

Pastrami

Add a few extra spices to your brine when curing beef and you have pastrami. Commercially prepared pastrami is taken from the boneless plate or the boneless flank, but the following preparation can be used on any cut of beef.

Prepare a mixture of the following ingredients.

1½ cups table salt
¾ cup brown sugar
1 teaspoon saltpeter
1 tablespoon pickling spices
½ teaspoon pepper
¼ teaspoon onion powder
⅛ teaspoon cayenne pepper
5 cloves, crushed
4 garlic cloves, crushed

Stir mixture into water until you reach an 80-percent solution (when it will float a potato or an egg). Prepare enough solution to cover the beef roast completely. Allow meat to soak in brine for three to four days per pound. Overhaul; cure several times. Wash and let dry before smoking. Cold smoke three to four hours, then finish cooking in your oven, or hot smoke until done.

LAMB AND MUTTON

Like pork, lamb is a meat that has traditionally been hard cured and consequently instructions for a hard cure are given here. Curing and smoking times can be altered to your taste.

Curing procedures are similar to those used for pork, such as brine in an 80-percent solution. A higher ratio of sugar is usually used when curing lamb, however. Garlic, onion, dry mustard, and pepper are spices that will nicely flavor this meat.

Thin cuts such as breasts, ribs, and loins need from ten to

fifteen days to cure. Normal-size legs and shoulders will require twenty-five to forty days to cure. Cure small—five to six pound—legs twenty-five to thirty days.

Wash and allow sufficient time to dry, then smoke at 100° to 120°F. for one to two days. If hot smoking, use a meat thermometer to indicate when meat is fully cooked. An internal temperature of 145°F. is required.

Thoroughly cured and smoked lamb is succulent and tasty, but if you prefer a faster way to smoked lamb, try working only with thin cuts. Rub dry-cure mixture into meat and smoke at 70° to 90°F. for one to four hours. Remove to cook, or hot smoke until done.

A better salt flavor can be gotten by curing thin cuts overnight.

VARIETY MEATS

Heart

Smoked heart is tasty with or without a cure. A rather dry meat, it lends itself well to slow cooking at the low temperatures of a smoker. Before doing anything with a heart, however, remove all fat, arteries, veins, and connective tissue. (These same procedures may be used on beef, pork, or any other heart.)

Dry cure or brine a whole heart for one to two days. If cubed or cut into strips, three to six hours will do for flavoring. Wash and dry after curing.

Lay cuts of heart on the open racks of the smoker. Cold smoke one to two hours, then hot smoke until fully cooked—when meat is tender when pierced with a fork.

A whole heart is especially good stuffed. Rub all surfaces of the heart with dry-cure mix, then stuff with the stuffing of your choice. Smoke at 200° to 225°F. until done. Cold smoking beforehand will not be necessary if you only want a mild smoke flavor.

Kidney

Veal kidneys taste best. Young beef, lamb, or pork kidneys are also good, but avoid large beef kidneys. They are often hard and have an unpleasant taste.

Kidneys are covered with a tough, white membrane that inhibits curing and smoking. If possible, cut this away before beginning; or alternatively, the kidney may simply be cut in half to expose the interior.

91

To prevent kidneys from curling in your smoker, run a wooden skewer through them lengthwise.

Whole kidneys should be brine cured for four to seven days, depending on size; if halved, for two days. Wash and let dry.

Hot smoking at 200° to 225°F. will take approximately forty-five minutes to one and a half hours, and will provide a mild smoke flavor. Especially if they have been halved, kidneys may dry out during smoking and curl up. A small wood or metal skewer can be put through them to avoid curling. Basting with vegetable oil will help preserve moisture.

Tongue

Beef, lamb, or pork tongues taste exceptionally fine when smoked. The smaller, younger tongues—those weighing less than three pounds—are best. But larger, five- to six-pound tongues are also good.

Tongue has a tough skin that inhibits curing and smoking.

The skin is difficult to remove unless the tongue is first cooked. Simmer tongue in water to cover for two to three hours, until tender, then peel and cut away the skin, also removing the gristle and other waste at the base.

The tongue may be smoked immediately or cured by allowing two days per pound. Smoke tongue for one to four hours at 140°F. Serve hot or cold.

Liver

The best way to handle liver is to cook it first and then cold smoke for a half to one and a half hours. Or try cutting liver into strips, curing two to three hours and then smoking.

JERKY

Use any lean butcher meat to make this traditional snack and trail food. The temperature used in jerky-making is not hot enough to cook meat, but serves only to dehydrate it. Therefore, if pork is used, it should be frozen under conditions that remove any worry of trichinosis. (See section on pork earlier in this chapter.)

Because the meat must be cut very thin, a sharp knife is essential, but you can save yourself the trouble by asking your butcher to cut the meat on his slicer. If you end up doing it yourself, choose a lean cut with a long grain running through it, such as flank steak. Lower-quality meats work well. Trim away as much fat as you possibly can (fat will have the tendency to turn rancid and spoil your jerky).

When working with a large cut, first trim it down to manageable size. A slab six to ten inches long and about one to one and a half inch thick is good. Working on the edge of this piece, cut slices that run parallel to the grain. Cut the pieces as thin as possible, preferably ⅛ to ³⁄₁₆ inch.

Slices up to a half inch can be used, but the thicker the cut, the longer the curing, smoking, and drying process and the greater the chance your jerky will spoil because all the moisture will not be removed.

If you have trouble cutting thin slices, place meat in the freezer just long enough to make it firm and easier to handle.

The primary preservative factor in jerky is the absence of moisture. Heating the strips of meat at low temperatures completely dries them without making them brittle. A salt cure aids in preserving the meat and adds flavor.

MAKING JERKY: Cut meat into thin slices, then into strips 1-inch long, then pat with dry-cure mix. Skewer each strip with a toothpick or hang the strips from the smoker's rack.

Meat may be lightly rubbed with a dry-cure mix just prior to smoking, or a more thorough cure can be used by soaking the strips in brine for six to twelve hours. The longer the cure, the stronger the salt taste and the better the chances of jerky lasting a long time without spoiling.

For smoking, arrange strips on smoker racks without allowing them to touch. Working with smoker temperatures of 70° to 90°F., smoke strips until they are completely dry. This usually takes ten to twenty-four hours. When jerky is sufficiently dry, it will break when bent.

To reduce smoke flavor, a period of heat without smoke can be used in an electric smoker.

Quick Jerky

If you don't want to wait for the lengthy curing, smoking, and drying times traditionally called for, this method will provide excellent-tasting jerky in a fraction of the time.

After cutting meat into strips, pat a coating of dry-cure mix onto the surface. The salt in the dry cure will immediately begin drawing moisture from the meat. You'll be surprised at how quickly the strips will literally be dripping water.

Drying and smoke-flavoring can be hastened by hanging the salted strips from the smoker racks. Poke a toothpick through one end of each strip and suspend it between the rungs of the rack.

Smoke the strips at 100° to 120°F. for two to four hours. This is a sufficient amount of time to provide a pleasant smoke flavor.

Remove the strips from the smoker and wash off the encrusted salt under a faucet. Pat meat dry with a paper towel and move them to your kitchen oven to finish the drying process. Set the oven at its lowest heat, often just marked as "warming." Leave the door ajar to allow moisture to escape and air to circulate.

Drying time depends entirely on the thickness of the meat. It will take a minimum of four to five hours. When thoroughly dried, the jerky will look shriveled. It will crack and possibly break when you bend it.

You needn't worry too much about storing jerky because it probably won't last that long anyway. But in case it isn't gobbled up quickly, simply secure a clean jar or coffee can, punch a few holes in the lid, drop in the jerky and place in the refrigerator. It will keep for months in this manner. Never store jerky in air-tight containers as the meat will soften and lose its snappy character.

PEMMICAN

This highly nutritious, compact food source is a natural to take along on camping trips. Since the basic ingredient is jerky, it has been included at this point.

Old-time pemmican recipes were simple enough, just calling for powdered jerky and animal fat. Today beef fat is usually employed and the mixture is made more palatable by the addition of dried fruit. Trailblazers with especially sensitive taste buds can also throw in nuts and their own blend of spices.

Begin your preparation by grinding up some jerky into a powder. Several runs through a meat grinder will do the trick. If you haven't got a meat grinder, use a clean hammer and pound the jerky to as fine a consistency as possible.

To the jerky powder add enough melted beef fat to make a thick dough. This will take roughly equal amounts by weight. Add whatever ground dried fruit you wish to the dough. While still warm, shape the mixture into balls or tiny loaves. Allow to cool and you're done.

Raisins are a good fruit to use. If you want to add nuts, they should also be ground. Flavor with pepper, especially if you choose not to put in fruit. Cinnamon enhances the flavor of fruited pemmican.

Pemmican will not keep nearly as long as jerky. After several weeks the salt begins to turn the fat rancid. By reducing or eliminating the salt in the jerky, you can extend the life of pemmican.

Store pemmican balls in plastic bags when out on the trail. An air-tight coating can be made by wrapping the pemmican in cheesecloth, then dipping it in melted paraffin.

CHAPTER VII

SMOKING POULTRY

By smoking poultry, you can add a fast and inexpensive way to enjoy smoked food. Since this low-cost commodity is a staple in many households, it's a perfect candidate for the exotically different flavoring that can be added by smoking. Substitute smoked fowl in any of your favorite recipes and discover its delightfulness for yourself. The cold meat is also fine eating and makes excellent sandwiches.

CHICKEN

Chickens are marketed in four sizes or ages:
Broilers—less than 2½ pounds
Fryers—2½ to 3½ pounds
Roasters—3½ to 5 pounds
Capons—5 to 8 pounds

As with most meats, the young animal is usually the best for flavor and tenderness. The only exception with chicken is the capon, which is often an older bird but one specially raised for eating. Capons have more body fat and a more even distribution of fat, which helps keep meat moist throughout the cooking process.

Aside from this exception, broilers and fryers yield the best smoked meat. Their small size means that even whole birds can be accommodated in the smallest of smokers. Often these birds come from the supermarket already cut into parts. Working with smaller pieces naturally takes less time. The advantages of working with a whole bird are for the attractiveness of the finished product on your dinner table and because smoking larger amounts of meat might just allow for some leftovers that can be enjoyed the next day. Regardless of the size you work with, the final taste is the same.

For a mild salt flavor in poultry, just sprinkle the bird with a dry-cure mix before smoking.

Cook, then Smoke

Adding smoke after cooking is best achieved with a roasted bird. If you have breaded, batter-fried, glazed, or in other ways coated the meat, it will inhibit the smoke flavor from penetrating.

To avoid drying effects, smoke at 70° to 90°F. Two to four hours will nicely flavor parts of a chicken. A whole bird should be placed on the racks of the smoker, breast up, and smoked two to six hours. Remember to provide a shallow pan to catch the drippings.

Curing

Unlike other types of poultry, chicken is seldom hard cured. Either the raw meat is simply rubbed with a dry cure or seasoned salt just prior to smoking, or it is given a brief brine cure of several hours. There is no reason not to cure chicken for longer periods, however. Twelve to twenty-four hours of brining will give a more uniform salt taste to whole birds.

Smoking

Smoke chicken at 100° to 120°F. For the short periods of time

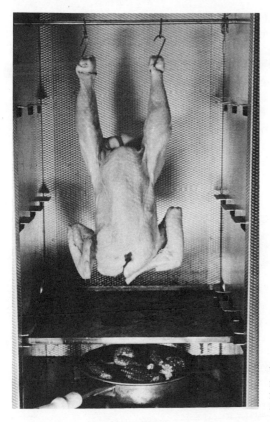

Whole birds can be suspended from the top of the smoker for a more uniform smoke flavoring and a more even browning.

you will be smoking, there is little danger of the meat becoming too dry. However, if you have an especially lean bird or if you are smoking parts, you can protect the moisture by basting with butter or cooking oil several times during smoking.

Parts or halves of a chicken will acquire a light flavoring after only one hour. Continue smoking up to four hours for a strong flavor.

To fully cook parts in your smoker, raise the temperature to 200° to 225°F. If these temperatures cannot be reached, 180° to 200°F. will do the job in a slightly longer amount of time.

Turn parts over once or twice during smoking if basting is necessary. The skin will turn a rich brown in color. When the chicken is fully cooked, the bones will pull apart quite easily at the joint.

If you are smoking a whole chicken, rubbing the bird all over with a dry-cure mix or seasoned salt just prior to smoking will give a subtle salt flavor. If the surface of the meat is too dry for the mixture to adhere, moisten it slightly. Smoke until the skin is brown, about two to three hours, for a medium flavor.

Your bird can be made ready to eat by hot smoking at 200° to 225°F. Place a meat thermometer in the thickest part of the breast or between the thigh and body of the bird. The tip of the thermometer should not be in contact with a bone. Smoke until internal meat temperature registers 160°F.

If your smoker is not capable of reaching temperatures above 200°F., smoke cooking is not advised. The amount of time required to cook the bird would be excessive and would result in drying the meat.

TURKEY

Turkeys are frequently given the full cure-smoke treatment. The meat of the turkey, which is on the dry side, stays fairly moist during smoking.

Moisture loss is relatively slow in any type of smoking or smoke cooking, the amount lost being a factor of time and temperature. Here is a typical example of how curing and smoking affect the moisture content of a turkey. A whole, dressed bird that is brine cured will gain about 5 percent in weight. Twenty hours of smoking at 110°F. reduces body weight by about 11 percent, due to loss of moisture. In other words, a fully cured and smoked gobbler will weigh approximately 94 percent of what it did when you started.

By comparison, if smoking is done at 140°F. for sixteen hours, the higher temperature will cause more moisture to be lost. The bird you started with would then finish at about 90 percent of its original body weight. In the higher temperatures of your kitchen oven, the loss of moisture is significantly greater.

Cook, then Smoke

Follow the same procedure as with chicken. An hour or two more of smoking time will be needed for large, whole birds.

Without a Cure

Sprinkle the bird lightly with seasoned salt or a dry-cure mix, then place on the racks of your smoker. Six to ten hours at 70° to 90°F. will provide a good range of flavoring. The turkey may then be oven roasted or refrigerated for cooking later. Roasting time and temperature are about the same as for a regular bird.

Use a meat thermometer and roast in a covered pan to preserve moisture.

Traditional Cure-Smoke

An old-fashioned turkey cure will take one day for each pound, up to a maximum of twelve days. Rarely is it necessary to go beyond that amount of time, even for birds over twenty pounds. These times will, of course, produce the strong salt flavor typical of a hard cure. For such lengthy cures, be sure to overhaul two or three times.

Most people will be satisfied with a whole bird that has cured only twenty-four to forty-eight hours. Depending on the thickness of the meat, twelve to twenty-four hours will suffice if you're curing parts. A brine cure is the most convenient way to cure all poultry. Wash after curing and hang the bird upside down to dry, allowing water to drain from the chest cavity.

For smoking, the turkey may be laid, breast up, on the lightly greased smoking racks, or preferably, suspended by its legs. Hanging allows for the best exposure of all skin surface.

Several times during smoking, baste the turkey, especially the breast area. Like all fowl, a turkey contains two very different kinds of meat—the tender, somewhat dry meat of the breast and the tougher, fatty meat of the legs. Conditions that cook one to perfection may not always cook the other properly.

One good method of providing a continuous basting for the breast is to lay several strips of bacon over it. These can be secured on a hanging bird with toothpicks. As smoker temperatures melt the bacon fat, it will soak into the bird, keeping it succulent and moist.

Bacon strips will prevent the skin from acquiring the desirable brown coloration of a thoroughly smoked bird. To avoid this, remove the strips one to two hours before the bird is scheduled to finish.

Smoke your turkey in a 120° to 140°F. heat for fifteen to seventeen hours. This smoking will produce deliciously flavored meat, but it must still be cooked before eating. You can accelerate the process and still get an old-fashioned taste by smoke-cooking your bird at higher temperatures. First place a meat thermometer in the thickest part of the breast. Hold smoker temperatures around 170°F. for eight to ten hours. The skin will turn a deep brown color. Follow this with a period of smoking at 180° to 200°F. until the internal temperature is 160°F. The bird

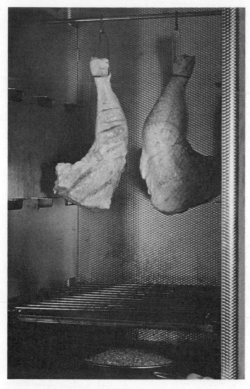

If the bird is too big to fit in your smoker, then just work with the parts.

will then be ready to eat and will be a mouth-watering treat served hot or cold.

In electric smokers too small to accommodate an entire bird, cut into pieces, working with a leg quarter or half the bird.

If you want to hasten the cooking process, or your smoker temperature won't go high enough, finish the bird in your oven.

DUCK AND GOOSE

Procedures for handling these birds are similar to those for turkey. To account for the smaller size of most ducks, use the lower end of the curing- and smoking-time ranges given for turkeys.

The flesh of duck and goose is considerably more fatty than turkey so basting is seldom called for on a whole bird. When smoking parts from which the skin has been removed, it may, however, be necessary to baste several times during smoking.

Either bird tastes very good when given the traditional cure-smoke described under turkey. Those who favor it without the strong salt taste can smoke after cooking (one to four hours) or cold smoke without a cure.

COOKING SMOKED POULTRY

If you finish cooking your turkey (or any lean poultry) in your kitchen oven, take measures to preserve the moisture. Smoking at low temperatures has provided you with meat that is unusually moist for fowl. If you use high oven temperatures to finish cooking or to reheat meat at some future date, you risk losing all that moisture. Simply tenting your bird in aluminum foil won't do the trick. If working with pieces, or a small enough bird, the entire thing can be sealed in aluminum foil, thus insulating it from the drying temperatures. Adding several tablespoons of water when you wrap the bird is an added guard. Cooking the fowl in a covered container is another way of conserving its moist character.

Remember that cured and smoked poultry meat may have a reddish coloration. This does not mean the meat is not fully cooked.

GIBLETS

Don't ignore the giblets when smoking your bird. Hearts, gizzards, and livers have an excellent taste when smoked and can make a delicious addition to any meal. Smoked livers can be turned into mouth-watering pâté; chicken and goose livers are the most tasty.

The easiest way to handle giblets is to cook them first. Gizzards should be diced; livers and hearts can remain whole. Put them into boiling water and simmer for one hour. Flavor them by adding regular or seasoned salt to the water. Alternatively, the giblets may be marinated overnight; use one of the marinades in Chapter IV.

To smoke, you will need a piece of metal window screen to place over the rack of your smoker. Rub the screen lightly with cooking oil to avoid sticking. One to two hours of cold smoking at 80° to 90°F. will give them a mild flavor.

PÂTÉ

Here's a quick and easy way to make pâté from any smoked poultry liver.

Cook and smoke about six medium-size livers. Dice the livers, then mash them together with a hard-boiled egg. When the mixture has been reduced to an even consistency, add just enough mayonnaise to make a moist paste.

Spread on crackers and enjoy.

STORAGE

Thoroughly cured and smoked poultry may be kept several weeks without refrigeration. Such storage, however, does make the poultry prone to mold growth, especially in the body cavity. The refrigerator is still the best bet for storage.

CHAPTER VIII

SMOKING WILD GAME

BIG GAME

Much of the game meat that reaches your table will probably be from large animals, and most of it from deer. The venison of the ubiquitous whitetail and the western mule deer counts among the most popular and flavorful of big-game meat. Smoking will allow you to enhance and vary the flavor of good venison and make older, tougher meat more fit for the table.

Curing and marinating offer countless new ways for you to enjoy your game. The extent to which you cure and marinate will depend upon personal taste and can only be determined by experiment.

Curing and Marinating

You may already be using a cure on your game without even realizing it, for many hunters, when faced with the strong odors of some game meat, soak their catch overnight in salt water. Removing gamy odors and tastes is only one reason for using cures and marinades. A second reason is to flavor, and a third—and sometimes the most important—is to tenderize. It's not hard to see how these two preparations can be used effectively on almost any game animal you bring home.

Curing is a good way to deal with the meat of older animals. After all, you can't put the whole thing into stew. The action of the cure will break down the tough fiber of the meat and make it more palatable.

Just as with butcher meats, there are many different ways to use cures on game, not all of which are, in the strictest sense, curing. Simply rubbing the meat with dry-cure mix or seasoned salt before smoking, for instance, is often all that is needed to give a subtle flavoring to good meat. Referring to Chapter VI will give an idea of how many different ways curing time can be varied to affect salt taste.

111

Since game meats will vary greatly in the amount of tenderizing, flavoring, and deodorizing they need, curing time will have to be tailored to the meat. A few experiments on small pieces should let you know what cures work best.

Here are some general guidelines that you should follow in the curing of big game.

CUT	CURING TIME	
	Regular Cure	*Hard Cure*
Chops and cuts less than 1 inch	6 to 10 hours	4 days
Steaks, 1 to 2 inches	12 to 24 hours	4 to 8 days
Roasts	1 to 3 days	8 to 12 days

Use the same time for either brine or dry cures, overhaul several times during curing, and remove all salt from the surface of the meat following curing. If rinsing in water is not enough, soak meat ten to fifteen minutes, then scrub with a stiff brush. Allow plenty of time to dry.

Use marinades to take the place of cures. They will remove odors, tenderize meat, and add the flavoring of whatever seasonings you put in them. Most game meat will require basting and a marinade can also work well in this capacity. After picking up meat juices in basting, the same liquid will nicely flavor gravies or stews. If you are unsure of how marinade will taste with a particular game meat, experiment. You'll often be pleasantly surprised.

Smaller cuts of meat are usually marinated six to ten hours; roasts take about twenty-four hours. It is not necessary to cover the meat completely with solution. To ensure overall absorption, turn the meat several times. After marinating, allow one to two hours for the liquid to drain from the meat before smoking.

Most persons find the fat of big game has too strong a flavor. Body fat is also the source of much of the unpleasant smell associated with some meat. If allowed to remain on the flesh, the fat will impart this strong flavor as it melts during smoking. For this reason, it is best to cut away as much of the fat as you possibly can.

One possible exception to this is a very young bear. The fat of a young bear is not as strong as that of other large game. It may be left on the meat without appreciably altering the taste.

Because all this built-in basting material is cut away, and because few wild animals have much fat throughout their meat anyway, basting is usually necessary. Butter, margarine, or cooking oil serve well. Bacon or salted fat pork may also be used, draped over the meat to provide continuous basting. The area covered with bacon is not as readily exposed to smoke. To compensate, remove bacon during the last hour or two of smoking.

Cook, then Smoke

This quick, reliable method is probably the one you'll use most often with your game. A delicious smoke flavor can be added to most cuts of meat in only one to two hours. For stronger flavor, or for larger roasts, smoke up to four or five hours.

Take the meat right from the oven to the smoker. Use bacon for basting cuts that will be in the smoker more than two hours; for others, baste occasionally.

Smoke at 100° to 120°F.

Cold Smoking and Hot Smoking

The wide variety of tastes in game meat allows such meat a wide variety of smoke flavoring. For the most part, smoking enhances rather than masks the flavor of meat. However, heavy smoking, especially when combined with a hard cure, will certainly strongly influence the taste of your game. This can be

A brief period of cold smoking after cooking is a fast way of flavoring game.

113

used to advantage as a way of saving poor cuts or of adding a new taste dimension to quality meat.

The cold-smoking times given below are for a range of flavoring that will suit the average palate. For a better understanding of the degrees of smoke flavoring that can be added to meat, see Chapter VI. Smoking directions from that chapter may be applied to big-game meat.

Cold Smoking Big Game (100° to 120°F.)

Cut	Smoking Time
Chops and cuts less than 1 inch	½ to 1½ hours
Steaks, 1 to 2 inches	¾ to 2 hours
Roasts	½ to ¾ hour for each inch of thickness

Meat smoked in this way must still be cooked before eating.

Smoke cooking big game is easy using temperatures of 200° to 225°F. If your smoker can't reach this heat, lower temperatures are acceptable—but below 200°F., it will take much longer to fully cook your meat. When possible, use a meat thermometer to determine when meat is cooked to your satisfaction. As a general rule, your game will be fully cooked when internal temperatures in the thickest part of the meat reach 160°F. Gauge when smaller cuts are done by examining them.

If you want a stronger smoke flavor, begin with a brief period of cold smoking.

Heart, Liver, Tongue

In some instances, these parts may well be the choicest meat you get off your game, and a good smoking will bring out the delicious best in them.

Prepare them as you would the same part from a domestic animal (See Chapter VI). The hearts of wild game are generally bigger than those of domestic animals, so slightly increased curing and smoking times may be in order. Tongue, especially, should be given a thorough curing and smoking.

Jerky

Any lean game meat can be made into jerky. Even lower-grade cuts will work well. If the meat is unusually tough, try slicing the jerky strips across the grain of the meat, as opposed to the regular, with-the-grain cut.

For superior jerky, use a better cut of venison. Cure and smoke according to instructions in Chapter VI.

Storage

Big-game meat may be frozen at 0°F. or less with little loss of flavor. The larger the piece of meat, the longer it will last without deterioration. Be sure to seal each piece securely in good freezer wrap. Improper wrapping will cause freezer burn and drying out of the meat.

Here are some approximate time limits for the frozen storage of smoked game meat.

Ground meat	3 months
Chops and thin steaks	5 months
Heart, liver, and tongue	5 months
Cubes and stew meat	7 months
Steaks	9 months
Roasts	12 months

Big-Game Characteristics

Curing and smoking times for all animals can be judged primarily by the size of the cut of meat you're using. Individual animals, however, have characteristics that may influence how you prepare them. Below is a list of the most commonly bagged big game, giving tips about handling their meat.

Antelope and Sheep. The pronghorn antelope and the bighorn and Dall sheep can be classed together for the excellence of their meat and no one could fault you if you were hesitant about tampering with their flavor. For a subtle taste difference that you're sure to appreciate, however, try a brief smoking of half to one and a half hours, after cooking. Mild cures also offer a good flavor variation.

Bear. The dark, coarse meat of this animal is fatty and subject to the trichinae parasite, just as is pork. Always fully cook or freeze under conditions that will make meat safe (see Pork in Chapter VI). The loin is usually the choicest cut. Roast the meat of younger animals. Braising or stewing is the best way to handle older animals that have developed tough meat.

All bear meat can benefit from a cure. Marinades are also good. Cold smoke roasts after cooking.

115

Deer. This most popular big-game animal provides one of the best smoked meats. Venison is excellent when simply smoked after cooking. Curing and marinating can also be used effectively to emphasize and vary flavor. Lengthy cures take too much moisture from the meat, so, unless you're preserving it, stick with flavoring cures or marinades.

The rump, shoulder, breast, or neck are good when braised; other cuts make good roasts. The liver and heart are very good eating. Cold-smoke or smoke after cooking. Smaller pieces may be hot smoked.

Elk and Moose. Although similar to beef in taste, the meat of these animals is darker and drier. Baste frequently or use bacon. Handle as you would venison.

Mountain Goat. In cooking your goats, follow the instructions for pork given in Chapter VI.

SMALL GAME

There seem to be two distinct categories of small game: (1) Those animals that nearly everyone considers edible; and (2) Those that most hunters would eat only on a bet.

Most everyone would put rabbit and squirrel into the first category, but the acceptance of other small game as table fare fluctuates widely between geographic regions and between individuals.

Nothing short of a gourmet chef will do more for your small game than smoking. Combined with curing and marinating, smoking will tenderize, remove unsavory tastes and odors, add flavor, and retain moisture. With the help of your smoker, you may just find that all small game belong in that first category.

 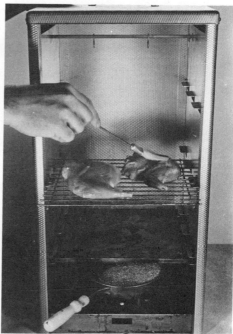

Nothing enhances the flavor of small game like a marinade. To prevent small game from drying out during smoking, baste it frequently with the marinade.

Curing and Marinating

Animals living in the ground often acquire a musty, gamy odor that causes people to turn up their nose at the thought of eating them. Soaking in brine is an effective way of combating such unpleasant smells as well as helping the meat in various other ways.

Almost any small game will taste better if cured in brine. Six to ten hours is all that is required to cure parts; small whole animals—such as squirrel—need twenty-four to thirty-six hours. Larger whole animals—such as rabbit or woodchuck—should cure twenty-four to forty-eight hours.

Savory marinades, such as those in Chapter IV, can also be used. Wine, which is a central ingredient in many marinades, offers an excellent complement to the taste of small game. When game soaks in a marinade of wine and seasoning, the subtle flavor of the marinade is absorbed into the meat. All alcohol evaporates during the smoking or cooking process, but

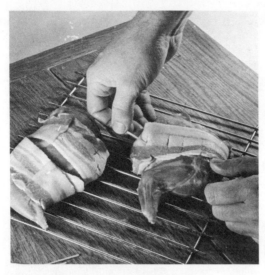

Lean game meat, such as rabbit, will have continuous basting if wrapped in bacon strips during smoking.

the flavor that remains is delicious, especially with rabbit, squirrel, or opossum.

Marinate parts about six to ten hours. Whole animals will have to soak eighteen to twenty-four hours. As with anything you're trying for the first time, it's best to make your first experiments on a few parts, rather than on a whole animal.

Basting

Rabbit and squirrel, the small game that will most often find their way to your table, are both very lean and will need basting. Butter or cooking oil will work, but, for an extra special touch, use a marinade containing dry red wine. Place a small pan beneath the smoking meat to catch the marinade runoff and use this liquid later as a flavoring in stew or gravy.

Bacon is also a good basting material for small game when simply draped over a whole animal during smoking. Wrap with strips of bacon and fasten with a toothpick.

Cook, then Smoke

A brief period of cold smoking after cooking is a reliable method of flavoring game. Smoking times of a half to two hours are usually enough for flavoring. Larger, whole animals will take up to four hours.

This fast method is also a good way of testing smoke flavor in meat. Say that you're looking for a way to spruce up the taste of woodchuck and have decided to try smoking. Cook the animal first with your favorite recipe, then take off some of the meat and smoke it at 100° to 120°F. just long enough to add a mild flavor. Compare the two.

Cold Smoking and Hot Smoking

Only you will be able to determine what degree of smoke flavor suits you best with each type of game meat. That will involve trial and error. The cold-smoking times provided below are based on the amount of smoke necessary to achieve a range of flavors for a particular size of meat. With small game, there are really only two broad sizes of meat to work with—the whole animal, or parts of the whole animal. In neither instance is meat very thick. For most palates, a half to two hours will offer a sufficient range of flavor with parts. One to four hours, depending on size, will flavor whole animals.

Use temperatures of 100° to 120°F. Meat must still be cooked before eating.

Because meat is never too heavy on small game, it can usually be smoke-cooked in a minimum of time. Temperatures above 200°F. are best, but lower temperatures will do the job in a longer time. It is difficult to use a meat thermometer on small game, so inspection of the meat is the only way to tell when it is cooked. Meat will turn brown on the outside and lose its raw appearance on the interior. It will also become firm and will be somewhat loose around the joints.

Small-Game Characteristics

The following list of the most-common small-game animals will give you a starting point for handling each type of meat. The body fat of all these animals can carry strong odors that will unpleasantly flavor the meat, so remove any excess body fat before smoking or cooking.

MARMOT. Handle the same as woodchuck.

MUSKRAT. This dark, fine-grained meat has a strong flavor. Use a long cure after which any smoking procedure is suitable. Stew or braise the older animals, fry the young ones.

OPOSSUM. Light, fine-grained meat. The opossum has a good distribution of fat throughout its flesh, making for a succulent meat. Remove excess fat, use a white-wine marinade or a cure on parts, then smoke-cook. Or cold-smoke, after which you can roast, braise, or broil.

PORCUPINE. Stay with the young animals. Parboiling tenderizes tough meat. Cure. Smoke before or after cooking. Frying or broiling are favorite ways of preparing this meat.

RABBIT AND HARE. The meat of hare is darker and drier than rabbit. Both meats are very lean and have a fine grain. They are especially fine with marinades, then fried or broiled, followed by a brief cold smoking.

RACCOON. This dark, coarse, fatty meat, which has a porklike flavor, is considered a delicacy in some parts of the country. Roast, then cold-smoke, or marinate parts, then smoke-cook.

SQUIRREL. Very lean meat that should be covered with bacon during smoking or repeatedly basted. Cure or marinate. Cook, then smoke.

WOODCHUCK. There is a big difference between young and old animals. Use a cure. Smoke-cooking will work well with young woodchucks; otherwise cold-smoke, then roast or braise.

WILD BIRDS

Many hunters have had bad experiences with cooking game birds and consequently relegate them to stews or some other method of vigorous cooking that successfully masks their flavor.

There are cooking problems inherent in wildfowl to be sure. Taste-influencing factors, such as the bird's diet and its age, have left their mark before you even bring it home. Quick and proper field dressing is also important. But regardless of these influences, all game birds are good fare for your smoker. Their naturally lean, dry meat lends itself to preserving or cooking at low temperatures.

If you consider that your bird can be smoked after cooking, or the raw bird can be cold-smoked or smoke-cooked, add to this the variety of flavor combinations possible with curing and marinating and it's easy to see how your smoker opens up countless new ways to appreciate wildfowl.

Curing and Marinating

Both of these preparations are useful for flavoring, but more important with some birds is how they can be tenderized and how unpleasant tastes and odors can be removed. Either curing or marinating will go a long way toward making birds of questionable quality more palatable. Old birds can be tenderized appreciably in this way. Of course, even tender young birds can benefit from these effects.

Cure game birds as you would domestic fowl. Brining is best. Simply place bird—or parts—in a crock, cover with brine, and weigh it down to keep the meat submerged. Cure small birds overnight, or six to ten hours. Medium-size birds should cure one to two days, and larger birds—such as turkey, duck, or geese—one to three days. Overhaul several times during the cure.

The size of the piece in question will also have some bearing on the length of the cure. Frequently, game birds are cut into parts—breasts, backs, drumsticks, thighs—or simply halved or quartered. Unless unusually large, parts can be cured in six to ten hours. Halves may take up to twenty-four hours.

Marinades can take the place of cures for those who don't want a salt taste. They don't have all the preservative powers of a cure, nor do they tenderize to the same degree, but they work wonders at seasoning your meat.

Whole birds are difficult to marinate, so it's best to work with parts. To determine how marinades can affect the taste of wild fowl, and whether or not they suit you, experiment with several parts of your next bird. Using one of the marinades from Chapter IV, or your own concoction, soak them for varying lengths of time and use different marinades, then smoke-cook them all for the same amount of time and put them to the taste test.

121

This method of preserving a bird's moisture is especially handy for wild birds. The heat of the smoker melts the bacon fat, providing a continuous baste.

Basting

No matter how you smoke a game bird, it will require basting. Unlike their domestic counterparts, wild birds don't have layers of fat throughout their flesh to keep them moist during cooking. Consequently, you have to take greater care to keep the meat from drying out. For meat that will only spend a brief time in the smoker, basting with butter, margarine, or cooking oil will do the job. Birds that need special attention can be covered with bacon. Old birds will certainly need special attention, also birds that are especially lean, parts from which the skin has been removed, and almost any whole bird that will be in the smoker for an extended period of time.

To use bacon, drape the strips over the entire bird, just over the breast, or tuck them between thighs and breast. For birds suspended in the smoker, secure the bacon with toothpicks. Remove the bacon toward the end of the smoking period to allow skin to color.

Giblets

When dressing your bird, be sure to save the heart, gizzard, and liver. These tasty morsels should be simmered until done and then smoked. (See Giblets in Chapter VII.) Simmering wild-bird giblets not only prepares them for smoking, but produces a savory stock that will come in handy in whatever recipe you use to cook your bird. Wings, necks, and even tough thighs can be simmered along with the giblets to produce this broth. The reason this liquid is so important with wildfowl is that the birds give up so little fat while cooking. The stock derived from the giblets is a natural for gravies, stuffing, or any necessary flavoring chore.

Smoke giblets at 100° to 120°F. for one to two hours. Dice the finished product for gravy or stuffing, make livers into pâté, or create exotic hors d'oeuvres.

Cook, then Smoke

Many cookbooks call for wildfowl to be roasted, broiled, or braised. Birds prepared in any of these ways may then be cold-smoked at 70° to 90°F. for one to four hours. This time range provides a mild to strong flavoring.

Cold Smoking and Hot Smoking

If you have not cured your meat, rub it with seasoned salt before smoking. Spread parts, flattened small birds, or intact whole birds out on the oiled smoking racks. Smoke at 70° to 90°F. for one to four hours. The skin will turn a light brown. Remove and cook or finish cooking with a hot smoke.

Raise smoker temperature to 200° to 225°F. to smoke-cook. A meat thermometer should be used in whole birds to determine when they are done. Pieces, however, will have to be inspected. Incidentally, the tendons of a wild bird are stronger than those of a domestic bird. Twisting the leg to see if the joint comes apart is not a valid way of testing if a wild bird is cooked. Instead, press the meat to see if it is firm; also inspect the interior.

If you start your bird at a high smoker temperature, it may be cooked before it has had enough smoke. A preliminary cold smoking will strengthen the flavor.

Inspect meat periodically to check for drying. Baste several times before smoking. Lay bacon over whole birds or especially lean pieces. There will be little or no drippings from your bird, but a shallow drip pan is still a good precaution, if only to catch the basting runoff. Marinades are excellent to use for basting.

Storage

Usually the problem with game birds is that they do not contain enough meat. If you should be so fortunate as to have a surplus, it may be frozen without loss of flavor. Because there is so little salted fat to become rancid, cured wild birds hold up better under freezing than do cured domestic birds.

Small game birds can be filleted by removing meat from the breast.

Game-Bird Characteristics

The following is a list of common game birds, with individual characteristics and suggestions on preparation. A general rule applicable to all species is that young birds are far superior to old birds. They're more tender, flavorful, and have more body fat. Old birds may be tenderized by parboiling. They can usually benefit from curing.

Another characteristic shared especially by older and smaller birds is that the meat of the legs can be very tough and laced with tendons. In such a case, simmer legs with your giblets for making stock.

DUCK, GOOSE. These birds are smaller and much leaner than their domestic relatives, but cooked in your smoker, their dark meat will turn out moist and appetizing. The strong fishy odor of some birds can be removed by skinning, curing, or marinating. If time is a factor, roast first, then cold-smoke for flavor.

PHEASANT. This meat is light, lean, and fine-textured. Older birds may be much tougher and their meat stringy. Make older birds more appetizing by boning them, then curing and hot smoking. Even young, plump birds will require basting. Their meat tastes good when well cured and smoked, or try a cold smoke, then roast in your oven.

TURKEY. Like domestic turkey, it has a fine flavor when hard cured (see the Traditional Cure-Smoke section for turkeys in Chapter VII).

GROUSE, QUAIL. Both have lean meat—that of the quail white, that of the grouse dark. Cut into parts and hot-smoke after a light cure. Try quail with marinades.

PIGDEON, DOVE. Like all smaller birds, these should be spread open and flattened. The dark meat of these birds is tasty, although that of the pigeon is sometimes tough. Curing and marinating work well with these birds. Cold-smoke for flavor, then braise.

CHAPTER IX

MAKING
AND
SMOKING
SAUSAGE

Combine any butcher or game meat with lots of salt and seasoning, pack it into a casing, add your own smoke flavoring, and you have one of the most delicious meat preparations ever devised—sausage!

Sausages come in every imaginable form, spiced for every imaginable palate. Both smoked and unsmoked sausages are available commercially. You can easily flavor fresh or cooked sausages from the store with just one or two hours of cold smoking. But, with less trouble than you imagine, you can make your own smoked sausage from scratch.

DO IT YOURSELF

Few things will make you more popular with friends and relatives than preparing homemade sausage. Once the word gets out, the demand will far exceed the supply.

Sausage preparation has always been a problem because specialized stuffing equipment was needed and the necessary casings were often difficult to obtain. If you plan to get into sausage making in a big way, then you should certainly invest in this equipment. On the other hand, if you only want to be an occasional sausage maker, a perfectly acceptable product can be made without any elaborate equipment. The items listed here are all that you will need:

Meat grinder—with a ½- or ⅜-inch plate and a ⅛-inch plate
Muslin for casings
Large mixing bowl
Wooden spoon
String

Making a Sausage Casing

One thing you cannot do without is a casing in which to stuff your meat. Traditionally, sausage casings were the intestines of domestic animals. More recently, plastic and edible plastic casings have been used. These casings may provide for an attractive sausage, but their use presents many problems for the novice sausage maker. We can dismiss their use here solely because they must be used with sausage-stuffing equipment.

A simple, effective casing can easily be made from unbleached muslin. For a finished sausage about ten inches long—a good size for most smokers—start with a piece of muslin thirteen inches in length by eight inches in width. Tear rather than cut the cloth. (Tearing produces a frayed edge, eliminating the countless tiny threads produced by cutting that would end up sticking to the sausage.)

Muslin sausage casing.

Fold the piece of muslin in half crosswise, so that you now have a piece thirteen by four inches. Leaving the proper, or selvage, edge of the cloth as the opening of the casing, sew along the frayed edge about a quarter inch from the edge. When you get to the frayed end of the casing, sew it closed in a curve, approximating the rounded end of a sausage, also keeping a quarter inch from the edge. This will eliminate sharp corners that might prove difficult to fill and that could leave air pockets.

When finished sewing, turn casing inside out, and you are done. Casings can be made in almost any size. If they are too long, however, they may not fit in your smoker. If they are too thick, then smoking and drying times will be unnecessarily prolonged.

Casings should be put in water, then wrung out just prior to being stuffed.

SAUSAGE VARIETIES

Most sausages are made either from beef (sometimes veal) or

pork or from a combination. The enormous range of possible tastes is determined by how they are prepared and what spices are used to flavor them. Aside from seasoning, sausage flavor will also vary by the type of meat(s) used, the proportion of fat to lean, whether meat is cured, and whether the sausage is smoked. Sausages may also be raw or cooked, dry or semidry. All of these distinctions will become clearer as the preparations are described.

In spite of what you may have heard about some types of sausage being the garbage pail for butcher scraps, it really does not pay to use low-quality meats. Making sausage is going to take time and effort on your part, so why jeopardize it. This is not to say that you should go broke buying choice cuts for your sausage. Recipes often call for "trimmings," the small pieces of meat and fat left over when a carcass is cut up, which can be combined with better-quality lean meat to arrive at the proper ratio of fat to lean.

Included here are recipes and instructions for preparing three different types of smoked sausage. Once you have read through all of these instructions and tried your hand at making some sausage, you can begin to create your own concoctions, varying those items just mentioned that affect flavor.

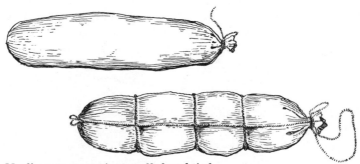

Muslin sausage casing, stuffed and tied.

Take all precautions whenever working with pork. Cold smoking alone does not take the place of cooking. The danger of trichinosis is not removed until the meat is heated to 137°F. *throughout.* Pork may also be made safe by various freezing conditions. For these, check the section on pork in Chapter VI.

Pork Sausage

In pork sausage, the ratio of fat to lean should be about one to two. If the fat content gets too much above this level the sausage will be too rich and there will be excessive loss during cooking. If much less fat is used, the sausage will be too dry.

Here are the ingredients you will need for an old-fashioned pork sausage.

    5 pounds pork (containing the proper fat to lean ratio)
    3 tablespoons salt
    5 teaspoons ground sage
    2½ teaspoons pepper
    1¼ teaspoons sugar
    ½ teaspoon ground cloves
    ½ cup cold water

First grind the meat through the ½- or ⅜-inch plate of the grinder. Mix all seasonings and sprinkle over ground meat. Regrind meat through the plate with ⅛-inch holes. Add water to meat and knead until the mixture becomes like a pasty dough. The meat is now ready to stuff into casings.

Wet the muslin casings and wring until damp before stuffing. Spoon ground meat into the casings, pushing it tightly into place with a wooden spoon and forcing it to fill every bit of the casing. Use your fingers on the outside of the casing to pack the meat. Packing should be done carefully; if an air pocket is left in the casing, you run the risk of spoilage.

When you have filled the casing, squeeze the opened end together slightly below the level of the meat. Forcing out a bit of sausage mixture will ensure a snug seal. Twist the muslin tightly and tie it with string. Large sausages can be given added support by tying the string around them at several points.

The next step is to hang the sausages in your refrigerator for at least twenty-four hours. This is a curing and drying period and should not be rushed. If anything, a longer, rather than a shorter, period is called for.

Smoke pork sausage at temperatures between 70° and 90°F., until it turns a deep mahogany in color. This will take twelve to fourteen hours.

Pork sausage is most tasty when sliced and fried.

Bologna

    3 pounds lean beef
    2 pounds pork (containing about equal parts fat to lean)
    5 teaspoons salt

2½ teaspoons pepper
1 teaspoon coriander
1 teaspoon thyme
¼ teaspoon saltpeter (optional)
2 cups cold water

Grind meat through the coarse plate of your grinder, then mix in all seasonings and regrind through the ⅛-inch plate. Knead the ground meat and water together until all the water is absorbed.

Some recipes call for the use of cured beef in bologna. To give it a try, simply grind the beef separately through a coarse plate, then knead in three teaspoons of salt and allow it all to cure about twenty-four hours before making your sausage.

Bologna should be stuffed just as pork sausage. Pack the meat tightly into the damp casings and tie them off with sturdy string or light twine.

Whether or not you have used cured beef, your sausage must now undergo a curing period before you can smoke it. The salt included in the recipe actually performs a dry cure inside the casing. Curing time is also drying time. Allow the sausage to hang in your refrigerator for eight to ten hours.

Smoke at 110° to 120°F. for about two hours. The sausage casing will turn a dark mahogany color, signaling it is ready for the final step.

Have a kettle of water, large enough to hold your sausage or sausages, already heated to 170° to 190°F. Put the sausage into the water and allow it to simmer. This cooking procedure will take anywhere from fifteen to sixty minutes, depending upon sausage size. If your pot is big enough, the sausage will float when it is thoroughly cooked. You can also test it by squeezing the casing between your thumb and forefinger, then quickly releasing the pressure. If it squeaks, it is done.

Summer Sausage

This dried sausage was originally made to survive long periods of nonrefrigerated storage. Prepared in the winter it would last throughout the summer, and thus its name. Considerable time is required to achieve the delicious flavor of summer sausage. The ingredients are as follows:

3 pounds lean beef
2 pounds pork (half fat and half lean)
5 teaspoons salt

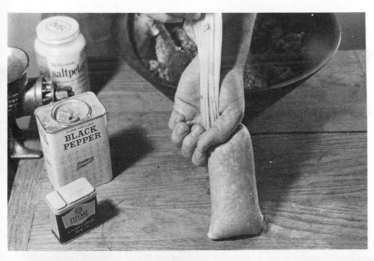

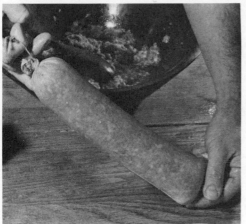

MAKING BOLOGNA. Turn the muslin sausage casings inside out (opposite, above) so that the frayed edge is on the inside. Remember to wet the casings before stuffing them. Use a large mixing bowl for preparing the bologna mixture (opposite, center). Mix in all the spices before adding water. Water is quickly absorbed by the ground meat, giving it a mushy consistency (opposite, below). Once you have some meat in the casing, force it to the bottom by squeezing it with your hand (top). This pressure will tightly compact the meat. A well-stuffed sausage (left), it is now ready for an overnight drying period in the refrigerator. After smoking, bologna must be cooked in 170°-190°F. water (right). Cooking takes anywhere from fifteen to sixty minutes; the sausage will float to the surface when it is done.

5 teaspoons pepper
1 teaspoon garlic powder
1 teaspoon coriander
½ teaspoon thyme
2 cups cold water

Coarse-grind the beef and pork, sprinkle the mixture with the salt, and regrind it through the coarse plate. Spread out the meat in an enameled or plastic pan and allow it to cure for some twenty-four to thirty-six hours in your refrigerator.

At the end of this period, mix the seasoning ingredients with the meat and grind through the ⅛-inch plate. Knead in the water and you are ready to stuff. Follow the stuffing procedure as outlined above.

A drying period of at least forty-eight hours is required before smoking. Hang the sausage in the refrigerator for this amount of time.

Cold-smoke summer sausage for twelve to fourteen hours in the temperature range of 70° to 90°F. The casing will turn a dark mahogany.

Considerable shrinkage will have occurred by this time. This type of sausage will lose 50 percent or more of its weight due to loss of moisture. What started out as a stuffed casing three or three and a half inches in diameter can easily be down to two inches by the end of the procedure.

There is one more vital step before you can sink your teeth into your summer sausage. *It must be aged.* A minimum of ten days is necessary; twenty is better. To age, simply hang the sausage in your refrigerator and forget about it until the time is up.

After aging, your sausage will be ready to eat. It will be a real hit for snacking or it can be incorporated into your menu in salads, omelets, or any other way your imagination can devise.

STORAGE

Under refrigeration, bologna and pork sausage will last only as long as regular cured and smoked meats—one to three weeks. For longer storage, pork sausage may be frozen for up to three months. Bologna will not keep its flavor under freezing.

Wild Game Sausage

Any game meat can be substituted for beef in sausage recipes. You will have the most luck with venison, which produces a very flavorful sausage. Use the same amount of pork and pork fat called for and add venison one for one in place of beef.

Personalized Sausage

All of the unique, exotic-tasting sausages in the world came about because someone had his own idea of how a sausage should be made. Undoubtedly, you will also come up with your own idea of how to improve and adapt these recipes. Of course, a little experience helps. Learning how heat, smoke, salt, and seasoning affect flavor will give you a better idea of how to tailor recipes and preparations to your own tastes.

A few basics that will come in handy:

The fat to lean ratio is important in sausage. The usual range is 25 to 35 percent fat.

Water is added to sausage primarily to make it cohesive. Without water, the sausage would crumble easily when you tried to slice it. Other liquids, such as broth or wine, may be substituted for water. Do not overdo the liquids, however, or it will take forever for your sausage to dry.

Several different ways of using salt were indicated in the preceding recipes. Use them as a guide.

The following is a list of spices that repeatedly crop up in traditional sausage recipes:

bay leaf, pulverized	ginger	pepper—black, white, red
clove, powdered	mace	sage
coriander	marjoram	savory
garlic powder	nutmeg	thyme
	onion powder	

Curing and spicing meats takes time. Allowing sufficient time for sausages to hang and age will help ensure a better-tasting product.

Always cook pork and pork products thoroughly.

Smoking time can be varied from a few hours of flavoring to the prolonged one or two days sometimes called for to heavily flavor and dry sausages.

CHAPTER X

SMOKING CHEESE, NUTS, AND EGGS

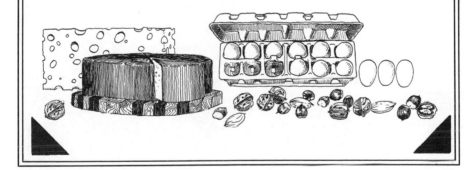

Almost everyone has tasted and enjoyed smoked meats, but few people realize how smoking can add interesting and exotic flavor to other foods as well. Cheese, nuts, and eggs are the traditional favorites. Some of these smoked foods are available commercially to a very limited extent, but making them yourself in your own smoker allows you complete control of the ingredients and their preparation.

If you're not convinced these foods would appeal to you with a smoke flavor, prepare a small portion and let your own taste be the judge.

CHEESE

Cheese is a delicate food that must be handled with care when smoking. Usually hard cheeses, such as cheddar, Edam, provolone, or Swiss are smoked. Of course, there are a host of other hard cheeses, including many imports, that are excellent choices for smoking. Softer varieties may be smoked, although their flavor is not always as compatible with smoking.

The first step is to remove all wax, rind, or protective wrapping. Cheese pieces should not exceed two inches in thickness. Slices are handy when smoking small amounts for individual meals or snacks. For larger quantities, cut the cheese into slabs or bars. Most commercially packaged cheeses available in the supermarket come in convenient-size cuts and are just right for smoking.

Smoke cheese at as low a temperature as possible; 70° to 80°F. is good. A light volume of smoke is *very* important. If smoke clouds too heavily in the smoker, it will result in the cheese having a sooty or bitter taste.

One to three hours of smoking offers a good flavor range in cheese. Watch for the characteristic amber color to appear and sample your cheese as it smokes to determine the level of flavor

141

Bars of cheddar cut to a good size for smoking (above). A piece of metal window screen over a smoker rack will allow you to handle even the smallest of items such as these almonds (below).

it has acquired. The smoking process will cause a small loss of moisture, resulting in a corresponding shrinkage and loss of weight, but all the nutrients will still remain in the cheese.

Whether refrigerated or stored at room temperature, cheese that has been smoked will not mold or spoil as quickly as unsmoked cheese.

NUTS

Nuts and seeds make a tasty snack when smoked. Almonds and chestnuts are especially good, but any variety can be smoked, including sunflower and pumpkin seeds.

Shells and skins must be removed from nuts before smoking. Canned nuts, already oiled and salted, can simply be spread out on a screen-covered rack and smoked. Nuts such as almonds will have to be blanched to remove their skins.

To blanch, simply pour boiling water over the nuts, then peel them. If skins will not come off easily, put nuts in a pan, cover them with boiling water and allow to sit for one minute. Pour off the water and remove the skins.

To add a salt flavor to nuts before smoking, soak them in brine. A simple 80-percent salt solution will lightly flavor small nuts in as little as five minutes. Depending upon size and desired salt flavor, nuts and seeds can be allowed to soak for six to ten hours. Prepare your first few batches with brief brining times, then adjust to taste.

For a zesty flavoring, add some seasoning to the salt solution. Soy or Tabasco sauce and onion or garlic powder offer an interesting variation in taste. Use small quantities, one or two teaspoons per quart of brine for the sauces, one half teaspoon per quart of brine for the onion or garlic powder. When used in combination, adjust measurements downward.

Cold-smoke at 70° to 90°F. As with cheese, nuts will acquire a bitter taste if the volume of smoke is too great. Smoke seeds for one to two hours; two to three hours will give a medium flavor to nuts.

To finish off your nuts or seeds in grand style, roast them in your kitchen oven. Spread a thin layer of nuts on a cookie sheet and place in a 300° F. oven. As they begin to brown, turn them frequently to avoid burning. A small quantity of vegetable oil or butter may be used on the nuts as they roast. Roasting will take about ten to fifteen minutes. If desired, sprinkle with salt when done.

Nuts may also be roasted in a heavy iron skillet. Heat a small quantity of oil in the skillet, about two tablespoons per cup of nuts, then add nuts and stir constantly until evenly browned. Spread nuts on paper towels to drain.

EGGS

Smoked, hard-boiled eggs are another traditional favorite that is easy to prepare.

After the eggs have been boiled and allowed to cool, arrange them on the screen-covered racks of your smoker and cold-smoke at 70° to 90°F. until they turn a deep amber color.

Eat them as is; include them in salads; or add them to your favorite recipe.

APPENDICES

APPENDIX 1
RECIPES

For the most part you'll be able to substitute smoked foods directly into your favorite recipes without any problems. Keep in mind, however, that hot smoking cooks food. If temperatures are high in your smoker, meat will emerge partially or fully cooked and you may have to make alterations in your recipes.

Another factor to remember is the salt content of meats that have been cured. You may wish to eliminate other sources of salt from a recipe, or even soak or simmer your cured meat to reduce its salt content.

Marinated meats can also influence the flavor of your recipes. Marinades impart a spicy flavoring to meats which, in turn, can be transferred to whatever dish you're preparing. It's seldom a big problem but should be considered if the subtle flavor of some celebrated dish might be ruined by the wrong spice seeping from your meat during cooking.

Some recipes tend to subdue the smoke flavoring you've worked so hard to produce. Either it's diminished by cooking or masked by the strong flavor of other ingredients. You can sometimes compensate for such problems by longer smoking times. You may have to produce a smoked product with a stronger flavoring than you like, just so the smoke taste will survive a particular recipe.

This section includes some easy recipes using smoked food.

SMOKED FISH CHOWDER

¼ pound bacon or salt pork, diced

2 cups smoked fish, diced

4 medium potatoes, peeled and sliced

2 onions, chopped fine

3 cups boiling water

2 cups milk

½ teaspoon salt

½ teaspoon pepper

3 Pilot crackers

Fry bacon or pork in cast-iron skillet until it becomes crisp, then remove it and set it on paper towels. Add smoked fish, potatoes, onions and cover with boiling water. Simmer for thirty minutes, or until potatoes are cooked. Add milk and heat for ten minutes. Season with salt and pepper. Just before serving, float halved Pilot crackers on top.

SEAFOOD SALAD

7 ounces smoked fish

1 can (6½ oz.) crab meat

1 can (6½ oz.) shrimp

2 tablespoons French dressing

1 cup celery, diced

½ cup mayonnaise

½ cup cucumber slices

3 tablespoons radishes, chopped

2 tablespoons lemon juice

Salt, pepper, and paprika to taste

Flake fish and crab meat. Remove black line from shrimp, then mix with fish and crab meat. Stir in French dressing and allow to soak for fifteen to thirty minutes. Add remaining ingredients, toss lightly. Serve over lettuce.

SMOKED CREAM OF SALMON SOUP

2 cups smoked salmon
2 quarts milk
2 slices onion
4 tablespoons butter

4 tablespoons flour
¼ teaspoon pepper
2 teaspoons salt

Rub salmon through a coarse sieve. Heat the milk and onion to scalding, then remove onion. Melt the butter, blend in the flour, pepper, and salt. Add milk gradually, stirring constantly. Add salmon and cook until smoothed and thickened.

SMOKED FISH PATTIES

2 cups smoked fish, chopped
   fine
2 cups cracker crumbs
½ cup milk

1 egg, well beaten
Pinch salt
Pinch pepper
Cooking oil

Combine all ingredients except cooking oil and form into patties. Heat enough oil to cover bottom of a skillet. Fry patties until golden brown.

NEW ENGLAND SMOKED CLAM CHOWDER

¼ pound bacon or salt pork,
   diced
2 onions, minced
6 potatoes, peeled and diced
1 quart smoked clams

5 cups water
3 cups milk
¼ teaspoon pepper
6 Pilot crackers

Render bacon or pork in cast-iron kettle. Add onions and cook five more minutes. Add potatoes and clams, cover with water, heat to boiling, and simmer until potatoes are tender. Add milk and heat to boiling; add pepper and Pilot crackers.

SMOKED OYSTER STEW

1 quart smoked oysters
Liquid from oysters
1 quart milk
2 tablespoons butter

1 tablespoon minced parsley
Dash onion powder
Salt and pepper to taste

Strain oyster liquid into pan; heat but don't boil. Heat milk in double boiler, then stir in hot oyster liquid. Add butter, seasoning, and oysters. Heat and serve.

SMOKED OYSTER STUFFING

1 quart smoked oysters
Liquid from oysters
1 loaf toasted bread, cubed
¼ cup milk

½ cup melted butter
Salt and pepper to taste
1 egg, beaten

Heat and skim oyster liquid, then pour over bread. Add milk, butter, seasoning, and egg, and mix thoroughly. Carefully stir in oysters, taking care not to break them. Stuff loosely in your favorite poultry.

SMOKED TURTLE SOUP

1½ cups cold smoked turtle
   meat
¼ teaspoon mace
1 bay leaf
3 drops Tabasco sauce

1 tablespoon lemon juice
2 quarts beef stock
1 hard-boiled egg white, diced
Salt and pepper to taste
⅓ cup sherry

Add turtle, mace, bay leaf, Tabasco, and lemon juice to beef stock. Simmer until meat becomes tender. Remove bay leaf and mace; add egg white, salt, and pepper. Pour in sherry after removing soup from stove.

SMOKED BEEF ON TOAST

½ pound smoked beef, thinly
   sliced
¼ cup butter
1½ cups milk
2 tablespoons flour
2 tablespoons dry, white
   sherry

1 tablespoon Romano cheese,
   grated
4 tablespoons sour cream
Dash salt
Dash pepper
1 teaspoon Worcestershire
   sauce

Melt butter in double boiler. Add smoked beef and heat thoroughly. Stir in flour, then add milk and mix well. Cook until smooth. Add sherry, cheese, sour cream, salt, and pepper, and heat. Just before serving, stir in Worcestershire sauce. Serve on toast corners or over baked potatoes.

SMOKED BEEF HASH

3 cups smoked beef, chopped
3 cups cooked potatoes,
   chopped
¼ cup milk
½ medium onion, chopped

1 egg
¼ teaspoon salt
Dash pepper
2 teaspoons cooking oil

Mix all ingredients except cooking oil in a bowl. Use oil to grease the bottom and sides of a heavy skillet. Pour hash mixture into skillet and press out to fill. Cook over low heat. Do not stir. After thirty minutes, it should be browned on the bottom. Finish off by baking at 350°F. for fifteen minutes, or until top browns.

SMOKED BEEF AND CREAMED CABBAGE

1 pound smoked beef, diced
1 medium head cabbage,
   chopped

1½ cups white sauce
½ cup bread crumbs,
   buttered

Cook cabbage in lightly salted water until tender. If beef is hard cured, soak it in water for thirty minutes. In a greased casserole dish, place alternate layers of beef and cabbage. Pour on white sauce and top with the bread crumbs. Bake at 350°F. for thirty minutes or until crumbs turn a golden brown.

SMOKED HAMBURGER DINNER

1 pound cold smoked
  hamburger
1 medium onion, chopped
1 green pepper, chopped
4 cups whole corn

½ cup bread crumbs,
  buttered
2 tomatoes, thinly sliced
2 tablespoons vegetable oil
Salt

Sauté onion and pepper in vegetable oil. Add ground beef and brown. Mix in salt. In a large casserole dish, place two cups of corn, then cover with half the meat mixture followed by a layer of tomato slices. Add a second layer of corn, meat, and tomatoes. Top with the buttered bread crumbs and bake for forty-five minutes at 375°F.

SMOKED HAM CASSEROLE

3 cups smoked ham, diced
¼ cup butter
2 tablespoons flour
2 cups milk
1 cup cheddar cheese, grated

3 cooked potatoes, sliced thin
1 pound cooked green beans
1 cup whole-wheat bread
  crumbs

Melt butter, add flour, then slowly stir in milk. Add cheese and heat until it melts. Arrange potatoes in a greased casserole dish and cover with green beans. Spread ham over potatoes and beans, then pour on the sauce. Sprinkle bread crumbs over the top. Bake for forty-five minutes at 350°F.

SMOKED HAM TIMBALE

2 cups smoked ham, ground
1 cup white sauce

2 eggs, beaten
¼ teaspoon dry mustard

Combine all ingredients and pour into a shallow, greased baking dish. Place dish in pan of hot water. Bake at 350°F. for fifty minutes, or until mixture is firm at center.

SMOKED HAM AND GREEN BEANS

3 pounds smoked ham	¼ teaspoon pepper
1 quart green beans	Salt
5 medium potatoes	

Cover ham with water and simmer over low heat for two to three hours, adding water periodically to keep at least one quart. Wash beans and break into one-inch pieces. Peel and quarter potatoes. Add beans and potatoes to ham. Cook about twenty-five minutes. Season and serve hot.

A tasty variation of the above recipe is made by adding scorched flour to thicken the broth before serving. Stir three tablespoons of flour into a heavy pan until it turns a golden brown, then stir into mixture and cook several minutes before serving.

SCHNITZ UND KNEPP
(DRIED APPLES AND DUMPLINGS WITH HAM)

2 pounds smoked ham	4 teaspoons baking powder
2 cups dried sweet apples, sliced	1 teaspoon salt
2 tablespoons brown sugar	1 egg, beaten
Salt, pepper	3 tablespoons melted butter
2 cups flour	Milk

Schnitz (Apples—with ham in this case)

Soak the dried apples in water for at least three hours (or overnight). Cover the ham with water and boil for two hours. Add the apples. Cook one hour, or until apples are tender. Add brown sugar. Salt and pepper to taste.

Knepp (Dumplings)

Sift together the flour, baking powder, and salt. Stir in beaten egg, butter, and enough milk to make a fairly moist batter. Drop the batter by the spoonful into the hot ham/apple broth. Cover tightly and cook dumplings for fifteen minutes. Serve steaming hot on large platter.

BATTER-DIPPED SMOKED PORK

½ pound hard-cured pork
⅓ cup flour
¼ cup milk
1 egg

¼ teaspoon baking powder
¼ teaspoon cream of tartar
Cooking oil

Cut pork into thin strips or slices, then cover it with warm water and allow to soak for fifteen minutes. Drain meat.

Prepare batter by mixing all ingredients except cooking oil. Heat ¼ inch of cooking oil in skillet. Coat strips with batter, then fry in oil until they turn a golden brown and become crispy.

CURRIED SMOKED LAMB

2 cups smoked lamb, chopped
1 cup celery, chopped
1 tablespoon onion, chopped
¾ cup brown gravy

2 tablespoons cooking oil
¼ teaspoon curry powder
Salt to taste

Lightly brown celery and onions in the cooking oil. Mix in remaining ingredients and heat, stirring constantly. Add a small amount of water if too dry. Serve over rice.

PINEAPPLE TONGUE

2 small to medium smoked
   tongues, thinly sliced
1 pound crushed pineapple

½ cup brown sugar
1 teaspoon mustard

Add brown sugar and mustard to crushed pineapple and mix thoroughly into a uniform sauce. Place tongue slices in a neat arrangement (like a handful of playing cards) on a shallow pan. Pour the sauce over the tongue and bake at 350°F. for twenty minutes.

SMOKED TURKEY LOAF

4 cups smoked turkey,
  ground
2 cups bread crumbs (or left-
  over stuffing)
2 cups milk

2 eggs, beaten
1 small onion, chopped
½ teaspoon salt
¼ teaspoon pepper

Combine all ingredients. Place in a greased pan and bake for one hour at 350°F.

SMOKED VENISON STEW

2 pounds smoked venison, in
  half-inch cubes
2 tablespoons butter
2 cups boiling water
1 teaspoon salt
¼ teaspoon pepper

1½ cups carrots, diced
1 cup potatoes, diced
1 cup celery, diced
2 onions, chopped
½ green pepper, diced

Melt the butter in a large pot. Roll the venison in flour, then brown on all sides over medium-high heat. Add water, salt, and pepper and simmer, covered, about forty-five minutes. Add vegetables and cook for about thirty minutes, or until vegetables are tender. If stew is too thick, add some more water and heat for a few minutes.

SMOKED WILD DUCK FILLET WITH ORANGE SAUCE

6 to 8 fillets duck breast, cold
  smoked
6 tablespoons butter, melted
½ cup water

3 tablespoons flour
¼ cup dry, white wine
1 orange
Salt and pepper

Brush the fillets with half the melted butter and lightly salt and pepper. Place water in a shallow pan, then lay in the fillets. Broil ten minutes on each side.

To make sauce, combine the rest of the melted butter, flour, wine, and pan juices left over from broiling with the juice from the orange. Heat in a small pan and stir until smooth. Arrange duck fillets on plates and pour on the orange sauce.

SMOKED SAUSAGE AND APPLE STUFFING

½ cup smoked sausage, diced
½ cup baking apples, chopped
1 cup bread crumbs
½ cup hot water

½ small onion, chopped
¼ teaspoon salt
¼ teaspoon pepper

Brown, but do not fully cook the sausage. Do not drain fat. Stir in remaining ingredients and heat. Use as stuffing for turkey or wild birds.

BEANS AND SAUSAGE

1 pound smoked pork
sausage
1½ cups dry kidney beans
5 cups water
1 medium onion, chopped
½ green pepper, chopped

1 teaspoon mild chili powder
¼ teaspoon garlic powder
2 tablespoons flour
2 teaspoons salt
2 cups tomato puree
½ cup bean liquid

Boil the beans in the water for three minutes, then remove from heat and allow to soak for about one hour. After soaking, cook the beans in the same water for an additional hour or until tender. Pour off and save water.

Combine sausage, onion, and green pepper in a large frying pan and cook until lightly browned. Mix in beans, chili, and garlic powder, salt, puree, and ½ cup of the bean liquid. Cook over low heat, stirring frequently, until mixture thickens—about one hour and three quarters.

SMOKED CHEESE LOGS

1 pound smoked cheddar
cheese

8 ounces cream cheese,
softened

2 tablespoons Worcestershire
sauce

½ teaspoon garlic powder

½ teaspoon salt

½ teaspoon cayenne pepper

Paprika

Grate cheddar with fine grater. Mix with cream cheese in large bowl. Add Worcestershire sauce, garlic powder, salt, and cayenne pepper. Mix well. Divide into three equal parts and roll each into the form of a log. Roll the logs over paprika which has been spread on waxed paper. Wrap each log individually in waxed paper and store in the refrigerator.

APPENDIX 2
TROUBLESHOOTING
YOUR SMOKING PROBLEMS

PROBLEM	PROBABLE CAUSE AND SOLUTION
Bitter taste	Can occur in some foods when smoke concentration is too heavy. The oily residue that accumulates in smokers is very bitter. If it comes in contact with food it will transfer this unpleasant taste.
Bitter, pitch taste	Smoking with soft woods. Pitch and resins will accumulate on meat smoked with soft woods, such as evergreens.
Hard, dry meat	Too long a cure; too strong a brine. Too much salt can dry meat and make it stiff. Soaking meat in water will help. Excessive smoking time or temperature can dry meat.
Metallic taste	Meat has come in contact with metal while curing.
Mold growth	The usual cause is dampness. May occur in hard-cured meat stored for long periods of time. Surface mold growth does not mean the meat is spoiled. Scrub or trim off mold. A slight mold flavor may be produced in the surrounding meat, but it may still be eaten. Rubbing the surface of the meat with cooking oil will delay future mold growth. Mold may also appear on sausage casings. Wipe off with a solution of vinegar and water.
Mushy spots	Bruised meat. Occurs most readily with fish.

Not salty enough	Too short a cure; too weak a brine. Enough salt has not penetrated the meat.
Soggy meat	Too weak a brine. Meat has absorbed too much water. Excessive amounts of water in meat can greatly increase the smoking time and temperature necessary to cook meat.
Sooty taste	Deposits of smoke occurring when: two pieces of meat touch during smoking or meat touches side of smoker; or smoke is trapped in such areas. Meat is improperly dried and smoke accumulates on surface moisture.
Sour taste	Cured meats will sour if stored too long. Improper drying. Sooty condensations on meat may cause souring.
Spoiled, discolored spots on meat	The spot was not cured properly; perhaps it protruded above the surface of the brine during curing. Sooty condensation.
Too salty	Too long a cure/too strong a brine. An excessive amount of salt has penetrated the meat. Soaking meat in water will subdue the harsh salt flavor.

APPENDIX 3
SPICES, HERBS,
AND BLENDS

ALLSPICE
In South America it's called Jamaican pepper. Resembles cloves, cinnamon, and nutmeg all rolled into one. Delicious with shellfish, ham, and meatloaf. Good in meat marinades.

CINNAMON
This sweet spice was once used in concocting ancient love potions and perfumes. Sprinkle lightly on lamb chops before smoking.

CLOVES
Indonesians used to plant a new clove tree every time a child was born, thus keeping a running record of the population; when someone died, a tree was cut down. Add whole cloves to pork or ham brine. Sprinkle variety meats and fish before smoking with clove powder.

GINGER
A root that grows below the ground in Southeast Asia. Combine with salt and pepper for use in dry curing meat. Terrific with poultry.

MACE
Mace is the covering around the nutmeg seed. A dash of mace goes great in smoked oyster stew. It's also good in smoked chicken à la king and on lamb chops.

MUSTARD
Excellent with smoked hors d'oeuvres, fish sauces, smoked hash, hamburg dishes, and of course smoked hot dogs.

NUTMEG
Fine in chicken dishes, meatloaf, smoked fish patties, and with fillets.

PAPRIKA
Made by grinding dried pods of sweet-smelling red peppers. A truly classic fish garnish, also good for sprinkling on chicken before smoking. Adds flavor and color to all foods. Most paprika is either domestic or imported from Spain, but look for a true Hungarian paprika for a special effect.

CAYENNE PEPPER
Hottest of the hot. Be careful with this stuff or it will really light your fire! Test it out on seafoods: shellfish, stews, and fillets.

WHITE PEPPER
Not as hot as black, red, or cayenne pepper, but more aromatic. Use whenever you might not want red or black specks to show up in your food.

RED PEPPER
Again, use with caution. Not as hot as cayenne, but hotter than black.

BLACK PEPPER
If there was a king of the spices this would be it, the oldest and most valuable spice the world has ever known. It was used for preserving meats during the Crusades. Columbus was looking for black pepper when he discovered America. More pepper is consumed worldwide than all other spices combined. It's been used in everything and anything. It even aids digestion.

HERBS

BASIL
A mint-type plant originally native to India and Iran, but prized by the ancient Greeks among others. Sprinkle over lamb chops before smoking; flavor stews and chowders.

BAY LEAVES
One of the world's oldest herbs, once used to honor the heroes of the Greek Olympics. Especially good in brines made for such

variety meats as tongue or heart. Adds zest to smoked fish chowders.

CARAWAY
A tangy, sweet seed used mainly to flavor rye bread. Add to pork brine or sprinkle over pork chops before smoking.

CELERY
Seeds not from your run-of-the-mill stalk of celery, but from a related member of the parsley family. Add to fish brines or sprinkle over fish fillets before smoking.

DILL
From India. Very similar to the caraway seed. Adds life to fish brines and marinades. Good with lamb.

MARJORAM
Another member of the mint family. Brings out a distinctive flavor in anything. An all-around herb. Add to brine or sprinkle it lightly over food before smoking.

OREGANO
Native to the Mediterranean countries. Famous for use with pizza, spaghetti, and other pasta sauces. Excellent when added to oysters, clams, and shrimp. Livens up any cut of beef. Great with smoked meatloaf or smoked meatballs.

ROSEMARY
Dried leaves of an evergreen shrub native to the Mediterranean area. Big in poultry brining and smoking. Sprinkle on fish fillets.

SAGE
Big in stuffings. Great with pork. Stuff smoked pork chops with sage dressing for a delicious combination. Not recommended with fish.

SAVORY
Another mint-type leaf. One of the most versatile herbs in the world. Great with meat, fish, poultry, hors d'oeuvres.

TARRAGON
Sparks chicken, beef, and lamb.

THYME
One of the most popular herbs. Adds a pungent flavor to smoked fish stews and chowders. Fine with chicken.

BLENDS

APPLE PIE SPICE
A mixture of allspice, cinnamon, cardamon, and nutmeg. Sprinkle on ham before smoking.

BARBEQUE SEASONING
More than fifteen spices mixed together. Very spicy. Mix with ground meat for smoked meat loaf, hamburgers, and meatballs. Sprinkle over fish before smoking.

CHILI POWDER
Mixture of oregano and chili powders. Adds zest to smoked hamburgers, meat loaf, and meatballs. Season shrimp or oyster cocktail sauce.

CURRY POWDER
A blend of about fifteen spices. For smoked chicken, ham, and beef curries. Serve smoked shrimp curry over wild rice.

HERB SEASONING
A mixture of celery, basil, marjoram, tarragon, thyme, parsley, and oregano. Sprinkle over lamb chops before smoking. Baste in butter over smoked chicken.

MONOSODIUM GLUTAMATE
Not as bad as it sounds. In fact, it comes from natural grains such as wheat and corn and plays up the natural flavors in foods. Has been used for years in the Orient but some people seem to have a reaction to MSG characterized by dizziness, sweating, or even chest constrictions. The reaction does not seem to be at all serious, but such people might best avoid MSG for the sake of comfort.

POULTRY SEASONING
A mixture of sage, savory, thyme, black pepper, coriander, rose-

mary, and allspice. Delicious when rubbed over poultry before smoking. Also good with fish.

SEASONED SALTS
Garlic salt, onion salt, celery salt; any number of flavored salts may be used with great success. Ideal when additional flavor is wanted with hamburgers, pork chops, and other meat dishes.

SEASONING SALT
Blend of spices, herbs, salt, and monosodium glutamate. It brings out the natural food flavors in anything. May be used instead of salt with excellent results.

APPENDIX 4
TIPS ON
HANDLING
GAME MEAT

The average hunter is neither a professional butcher nor an expert meat processor, but he can still do a satisfactory job of field-preparing wild game. Any person can carry all the tools required to dress out big game and keep it in good condition until a refrigerator can be reached. Necessary items include a good knife and sharpening stone, a small axe, a hank of rope, and, if hunting in warm weather, a box of black pepper. A hunter who carries the above equipment, and who realizes why and how meat spoils, should be able to store meat in the wilderness for at least a week, even during summer.

The first prerequisite for quality meat is that the animal be killed quickly and efficiently. If a deer or elk is wounded and runs a great distance, its meat will acquire a dark, deep red-to-purple color, and will also become saturated with strong-tasting chemicals produced by the animal under stress.

After a kill, the very next step is to remove any musk glands the animal may have on its legs. This is very important. Otherwise you might get musk on your hands and then transfer it to various parts of the animal, even the exposed meat. Musk will spoil the taste of anything it comes in contact with.

Once the musk glands have been disposed of, immediately remove entrails, saving the heart and liver.

Internal body heat is the number-one spoiler of wild-game meat. It encourages bacteria to grow and thrive in the stomach and intestines, which, in turn will produce gases that force strong-tasting chemicals into the meat and emit the putrid odors associated with bloated carcasses.

After the entrails have been removed, remaining body heat may be dissipated by hanging the animal from a tree and propping the cavity open with sticks to allow air to circulate and cool. Always hang the animal by its head. This will also discourage blood from collecting and putrifying between muscle layers.

In warm weather, blowflies may present a problem. Blowflies possess the amazing ability to lay eggs that will hatch into maggots within a few short hours. To protect the meat against maggot development, save some blood from the gutting and smear it over any exposed meat. The blood will coagulate into a hard coating that will prevent the fly eggs from hatching. In the few areas where the blood will not dry, sprinkle black pepper to ward off the flies.

In deep wilderness, it's a good idea to smoke wild game before the long haul home. Cut it into large pieces, rub it with salt cure, or soak it in brine, then smoke on a stick smoker for one to two days.

Domestic animals are slaughtered and rendered under ideal conditions, always in the same fashion, with no loss of meat from poorly placed shots or careless handling. You're not going to have as good a record with wild game, but you can keep your losses due to spoiled meat to a bare minimum by studying detailed wild game manuals and using a little common sense in the field.

Elk and Moose

Split lengthwise with an axe after gutting. Cut halves into quarters and hang quarters high off the ground. If you're alone and can't raise the quarters, drape them over a blown-down tree. In warm weather, protect from flies and wrap in cheese-cloth and cotton meat bags.

Deer

Mule and whitetail deer are a lot easier to handle. Be sure to remove the scent glands on their hind legs. A 200-pound white-tail will dress out to about 100 pounds, of which 80 pounds will be actual meat for the smoker.

Bear

Make sure you have a small whetstone, or at least a steel—skinning and cleaning a bear will dull the sharpest knife in minutes. Remove every trace of fat you can.

Like pork, peccary, and wild boar, bear meat may carry trichinosis. Never let the bear's hair come in contact with meat. Always keep it cool, because the fat easily turns rancid.

168

Rabbit

Rabbit should be gutted directly after killing, skinned, and kept in a cool place (between 33° and 40°F.) for about twenty-four hours before brining or freezing. Always remove the scent glands under the front legs.

Rabbit, squirrel, and sometimes opossum, may carry the disease tularemia. You should look for white flecks in the liver and discard any animal with these telltale marks.

Squirrel

Should be gutted immediately after killing. Skin and rinse with cold water, wipe clean, soak in salt water for ten hours, and refrigerate until brining or freezing time, but no later than forty-eight hours after cleaning.

Raccoon and Opossum

Raccoon are fat, oily animals, suitable for eating only if killed during winter. As much fat as possible should be removed by trimming. Cut off the musk glands under the front legs and on each side of the backbone, toward the rear. Gut immediately after killing, skin, soak in salt water and keep refrigerated for at least twenty-four hours before brining or freezing.

The same goes for opossum, but boil the fat off in a pot of water instead of trimming it with a knife.

Woodchucks

Young ones are the only ones worth eating. Clean immediately and soak overnight in heavy salt brine.

Muskrat

Remove the musk glands on lower belly. Soak in mild salt water brine five to seven hours.

Grouse, Pheasant, Wild Turkey

Dress as soon as possible to help keep digestive juices from seeping into and spoiling the meat. You have a choice of skinning or plucking game birds. The above three birds should be dry plucked, because skinning will remove quite a bit of flavor and the meat will tend to dry out quickly when smoked or cooked.

Dove

Skin out the breast, soak in salt water for a few hours, then chill overnight before brining or freezing.

Quail

Perhaps the most fragile meat of all game. Should be cleaned and cooled immediately, and brined or frozen the very next day.

Duck and Goose

Some people say to hang and age waterfowl without gutting them. You could try it, but you'd probably be better off removing the entrails the same day you kill the bird. Do not skin or pluck the bird until it has been washed on the inside with salt water, patted dry, and hung in a cool place for thirty-six to forty-eight hours.

When cleaning strong-tasting waterfowl, such as sea ducks, it's best to skin them to get rid of unwanted flavors. Some authorities will tell you to dip birds in wax when plucking. That's a lot of nonsense; for the most part, it's still time consuming and messy. Pull the feathers out dry, by hand, by pinching and pulling.

APPENDIX 5
GLOSSARY
OF TERMS

Acids—Acidic liquids, such as fruit juices or vinegar, used in marinades to tenderize meat.

Blanch—Used here to describe a method of removing skins from nuts by scalding them with boiling water.

Braise—A method of cooking whereby meat is browned in fat, then simmered in a covered pan with a small amount of liquid. Appropriate for tough meats.

Brine—Any solution of salt and water. Traditionally, curing brines also contained sugar and saltpeter. Brines used in this book are at 80 percent solution.

Brine container—Any nonmetallic container used to hold meat curing in a brine.

Brine cure—The use of a brine to cure meat.

Brine mix—The mixture of dry ingredients that are combined with water to make a brine.

Butcher meat—Retail meats available in the supermarket, such as beef, lamb, veal, and pork.

Cold smoker—A food smoker designed specifically to cold-smoke food. For this reason, the heat source is in a compartment separate from the food. Smoke is channeled to the food through a pipe to dissipate heat.

Cold smoking—The smoking of food at temperatures below 120°F. Used to flavor and/or dry foods. A method of preserving meats.

Crock—An earthenware container used for curing. Any curing container.

Cure—To flavor or preserve meat by treating it with salt and seasoning.

Curing container—Any nonmetallic container used to hold curing meat.

Drip pan—A small, shallow pan used in a smoker to catch dripping fat or basting runoff.

Dry cure—A method of curing meat by packing it in salt and seasoning.

Dry-cure mix—The mixture of ingredients used in dry curing.

Egg method—A way of producing an 80-percent brine in which salt is added to water until it floats an egg.

Electric smoker—A smoker in which an electric heating element is used to heat wood until it smokes, and to maintain high temperatures capable of cooking food.

Fillet—A boneless slice of fish. A method of preparing fish for smoking in which the meat is cut from the bones.

Firecan—A can or bucket in which wood is burned to provide a heat source for a smoker.

Fuel—Wood used to produce smoke in a smoker.

Hard cure—A lengthy cure in which meat acquires a high salt content. A method of preserving meat by allowing salt to displace its moisture content, thus retarding the growth of bacteria.

Heat source—In a smoker, the source of heat and smoke, such as a firecan.

Hog dressing—A method of preparing fish for smoking in which the headless, tailless, gutted fish is flattened to allow for fast, even flavoring or cooking.

Hot smoking—Smoking at temperatures above 120°F. Smoking at temperatures hot enough to cook food as it smokes. Usually refers to temperatures above 170°F.

Jerky—Thin strips of lean meat that have been thoroughly dried. A traditional snack or trail food.

Marinade—A spiced solution, usually containing acid and/or oil, used to flavor and tenderize meat.

Overhauling—A method of reviving a cure in which meats are rearranged so as to allow different parts to be exposed to the effects of the brine or dry cure. In a brine cure, it also involves stirring the brine to mix in settled ingredients.

Parboil—To partly boil meat, usually in preparation for roasting. Used on tough meat.

Pâté—A liver paste, usually made with poultry livers.

Pemmican—A concentrated food prepared with a mixture of fat and powdered dried meat. Can also include dried fruit, nuts, or spices.

Potato method—A way of producing an 80-percent brine in which salt is added to water until it floats a potato.

Resalting—A required procedure when dry curing large pieces of meat, in which meat is removed from the curing container to receive a fresh application of dry-cure mix, then repacked for the duration of the cure.

Saltpeter—Potassium nitrate (sometimes sodium nitrate). In cures, it serves as an oxidant to color meat and aid preservation.

Sausage casing—Container to hold ground meat for sausage; the sausage "skin." Traditionally, the intestines of cattle or hogs were used. This book recommends the use of muslin casings.

Seasoned salt—A mixture of salt and spices used to flavor meat.

Smoke baffle—A metal plate in some smokers which disperses the flow of smoke throughout the compartment.

Smoke cooking—Hot smoking.

Smokehouse—A large smoker, traditionally, one used for cold-smoking meat to preserve it.

Smoker—Any commercially built or makeshift device capable of smoking food.

Smoking—Exposing food to smoke for the purpose of flavoring and/or preserving it.

Traditional cure—Hard cure.

INDEX

freezers, 3, 41, 73, 87, 115, 123
frog legs, 73
fruit, dried, 97
fuels, 25–28, 171

Game Marinade, 58
game sausage, 136–137
game, wild, 38, 109–126, 167–170
  age, 111, 112–113, 120
gamey odors, removing, 59, 111–
  113, 116, 117
garbage can smoker, 21
garlic, 46
giblets, 107, 122–123
ginger, 46, 161
gizzards, 107, 122
glass containers, 35, 47
goat, 116
goose, 106–107, 121, 124, 170
gravies, 59, 81, 118, 123
green wood, 27
grouse, 125, 170
gummy deposits, 25

haddock, 63
Ham Brine, 51
Hamburger Dinner, Smoked, 152
hamburgers, 78, 88
Ham Casserole, Smoked, 152
Ham with Dried Apples and
  Dumplings, 153
Ham Dry Cure, 53–54
Ham and Green Beans, Smoked,
  153
hams, 4, 38, 41, 47, 79–84, 86
Ham Timbale, Smoked, 152
hanging meat, 167–168
hard-curing, 41, 83–87, 90, 171
hard meat, 159
hardwoods, 25, 26
hare, 120
heart, 91, 107, 114–116
  stuffed, 91
heat, smoker, *see* temperature
heating element, 13, 14, 172
hemlock wood, 25
herbs, 39, 162–164
  seasoning, 164
herring, 63

hickory wood, 26
hog dressing, 64, 172
honey, 39, 45, 46
  cures, 45
honing knives, 33–34
hooks, food, 13, 14, 18, 38, 41
hornbeam wood, 26
hot dogs, 78
hot plate, electric, 14, 20, 21
hot smoking, 6–7, 36, 69, 88, 92,
  104, 172
  see also smoke-cooking
hunting trips, 23–24

iceboxes, 3
indoor use of smokers, 13

jerky, 45, 93–97, 114–115, 172

ketones in smoke, 6
kidneys, 91–92
knives, 31–34

lamb, 90–92
Lamb, Curried Smoked, 154
larch wood, 25
leftovers, smoking, 78
lemon juice, 46, 56
lime, 87
liver, 93, 107–108, 114–116, 122, 123
locust wood, 26
loin, pork, 83, 84, 86

mace, 46, 161
Madeira, 56
mangrove wood, 26
maple syrup, 39, 46
maple wood, 26
margarine, 113, 122
marinades, 39, 56–59, 111–112, 117–
  118, 120, 121, 123, 147, 172
  containers, 57
marjoram, 163
marmot, 119
masonry smokers, 21
meat, color, 40
Meat, Fatty, Marinade, 57–58
meat grinders, 40, 97, 129
meat thermometer, 36–37, 114, 123